AF412822

MAKING A DIFFERENCE

A CATECHIST'S GUIDE TO SUCCESSFUL CLASSROOM MANAGEMENT

Thomas P. Walters
Rita Tyson Walters

Sheed & Ward

Sheed and Ward™ is a service of National Catholic Reporter Publishing, Inc.

Library of Congress Catalog Card Number: 85-62390

ISBN: 0-934134-61-8

Published by: Sheed and Ward
               115 E. Armour Blvd. P.O. Box 281
               Kansas City, MO 64141-0281

To order, call: (800) 821-7926

CONTENTS

Introduction

1   **BEING A CATECHIST**   7

What Is A Catechist?
What Does It Mean To Catechize, To Hand
   On The Faith?
What Is Effective Classroom Management?
Why Is Effective Classroom Management
   So Important?

2   **SETTING A DIRECTION**   13

Where Do I Begin?
What Is A Textbook?

3   **CREATING A SPACE**   24

What Is A Classroom Supposed To Do?

4   **TEACHING A STUDENT**   33

What Is A Student?
How Can I Do All Of This?

5   **TEACHING STUDENTS**   40

Student Or Students — What's
   The Difference?

6   **BECOMING A CLASSROOM**   45
     TEACHER

What Do Successful Classroom Teachers Do?

7   **PREPARING A LESSON**   56

What Is Lesson Planning?

8 GETTING STARTED   67

What Do I Have To Do?
What Do I Do On The First Day?

9 HANDLING PROBLEMS   79

What Do I Do If A Student Misbehaves?
What Are The Principles?
What Are The Common Problems?

10 PULLING IT ALL TOGETHER   88

How Can I Keep It Going?

INTRODUCTION

This book is written for you, the parish catechist, whether you are about to enter the classroom for the first time or you are a veteran who has entered the classroom so often that you have lost count. Classroom management is an attitude as well as a skill. This book aims to develop both. Well-managed, "safe" religion classrooms do not just happen. They are created by catechists like yourself who know the type of classroom they would like to have and who possess the skills to make it a reality. There is no magic trick.

Catechists who are able to effectively manage classrooms are confident, understand the teaching/learning process, have a knowledge of their students, know the subject matter they are teaching and know the strengths and weaknesses of the environment in which they are working. Successful catechists have well-managed classrooms, and well-managed classrooms tend to produce successful catechists. You can be a successful catechist; this book can help you become one.

The book's purpose is two-fold. First, it provides you with a way of thinking about classroom management. Secondly, it offers practical suggestions for achieving a well-managed classroom environment, an environment in which both you and the learner feel safe and secure and in which teaching and learning can take place and be enjoyable. Everyone likes to be successful. Success is a sense of confidence and achievement that comes from having done one's job to the best of one's abilities. If you take the time to read this book and put into practice the suggestions made, you will be well on your way to becoming the successful catechist you want to be. Read on.

1
BEING A CATECHIST

When Frederick had finished, they all applauded.

"But Frederick," they said, "you are a poet!"

Frederick blushed, took a bow, and said shyly, "I know it."

Leo Lionni
Frederick

What Is A Catechist?

Frederick wasn't a catechist. He was a field mouse in a chatty family of field mice. But he was a special field mouse because he was called to a special task. While the other members of his family worked day and night to gather corn and nuts and wheat and straw for the long cold winter, Frederick gathered sun rays, colors, and words. Somehow he knew that these were going to be important, and they were. When the corn and nuts and wheat were gone, Frederick through his words was able to bring the warming rays of the sun and the beautiful colors of the blue periwinkles and red poppies to help his family survive the winter. Frederick, the poet, knew from the beginning what he was doing.

Before we can begin to talk about classroom management, you need to ask yourself what it is that you are expected to do as "catechist." Like Frederick, you need to know from the start what your role is. The term catechist is perhaps new to you. It certainly is not used in everyday conversation. And if the term was used at all when you were being recruited to help in your parish program, you, no doubt, translated it into religion teacher or "CCD" teacher. When people ask what you do in the parish, you probably say, "I teach." You are right. To be a catechist is to be a teacher, but a teacher with a special task.

The term catechist comes from a Greek word meaning "to echo." The church has the responsibility of handing on the faith, of echoing the Word of God, to its own generation and to succeeding generations. This is the catechetical ministry. In the early church if one assumed this task, he or she was called a catechist, a person responsible for echoing the message of Jesus to the community. Today, as in the past, people actively involved in the formal ministry of handing on the faith are called catechists. By choosing to become involved in your parish's religious education (catechetical) program, you became a catechist. You assumed the responsibility of handing on the faith.

What Does It Mean to Catechize — To Hand On The Faith?

If you're like the majority of catechists, this is one of your first questions — "What did I get myself into?" You feel totally unprepared for the task. "I'm not the person to walk into a classroom and tell people what they are supposed to believe." Good! Because a catechist is not a person who tells others what they must believe. In fact, if you did this you would not be catechizing.

According to the National Catechetical Directory, *Sharing the Light of Faith*, the purpose of catechesis is to help a person's faith become "living, conscious and active through the light of instruction." Catechesis concerns itself with both the discovery of faith and the faithful transmission of the tradition. And this cannot be done if your only concern is with telling the students what to believe.

Your task as a catechist is to echo the Word of God in such a way that the faith of your students may mature and the Catholic story may be faithfully handed on. This is done through an instructional process which provides opportunities for a student's faith to be discovered, named, nurtured, challenged and affirmed by the echoed message which is found in the scriptures and in the church's traditions. As a catechist you are responsible for both the faith of the student and the faith of the community. To fulfill this responsibility in the classroom, you must create an instructional environment which allows for both the development of faith and the handing on of the tradition. The creation of this type of setting necessitates your possessing the skills of an effective classroom manager.

What Is Effective Classroom Management?

You already have an image of what a well-managed classroom looks like, and it, no doubt, has a lot to do with the way in which you were educated as a child. It may even resemble the classroom of your favorite teacher. What is your image? Take a few minutes to think about it. Write it down on a piece of paper or in the space provided below. What do you see? What is the teacher doing? What are the students doing? What does the classroom itself look like?

My Image of a Well-Managed Classroom is . . .

Believe it or not, most people tend to teach the way they were taught. You're probably no different. When you enter the classroom, especially if you are not formally trained to be a teacher, you are going to fall back on what you know, what is familiar to you. The image you have just written may be your ticket to successful classroom management or a sure guide to failure. Let's take some time to analyze your image.

If you were educated in a teacher-centered classroom, your image may be one where all of the learners are seated in their desks with their hands folded and their eyes dutifully focused on the teacher. The teacher is in the front of the room and is talking to the class. This is a very common image. And its focus, the teacher, is one of the key elements in effective classroom management. But this is an incomplete image. There are four essential elements in effective classroom management.

Perhaps you imaged a classroom where the learners were actively engaged in various activities of their own choosing and were working in groups or individually. The teacher moved from group to group as a resource person. Again, a common image. You have centered in on the activities of both the learners and the teacher. But this image, too, is incomplete. Effective classroom management is the result of the successful interaction of four variables. You have identified the teacher and the learners. What do you think the other two variables are?

Reflect on your image and the two images given above. What is there to be concerned about in addition to the teacher and the learners? In the first image the teacher is talking. She or he is communicating a content. In the second image the learners are involved in activities, learning a content. This content is the third variable and is best described as the subject matter. Finally, in both images the teacher and the learners are interacting with the subject matter in a particular setting. This setting, the learning environment, is the fourth variable.

Teacher	Learner
Learning Environment	Subject Matter

Effective classroom management is the result of these four variables working together so that the teacher teaches and the learners learn. In your situation, you, as catechist, are the teacher, your students are the learners, the subject matter is to be found in your textbook series, and your classroom is the learning environment. As a classroom catechist you have the task of creating an instructional environment in which the faith of the learners may develop through planned activities based on the scriptures and traditions of the Catholic Christian community.

Why Is Effective Classroom Management So Important?

One of the chief reasons teachers in any subject area give for leaving the classroom after one, two, or more years of teaching is problems with classroom management. Many individuals who have high ideals, strong intellectual ability, and a love of teaching leave their professions simply (or not so simply) because managing the classroom is more than they can handle. The reason parish catechists, like yourself, leave is no different.

Based on interviews with both volunteer catechists who have been in the classroom for more years than they care to remember and those whose stay was short-lived, we have found that the failure to gain and to maintain effective control in the classroom setting is the major cause of their giving up and throwing in the towel. Because they were ineffective classroom managers, these well-intentioned and talented individuals never had a chance to discover if they were effective catechists.

In Conclusion

If you are concerned about whether or not you can effectively manage a classroom, you're on the right track. Effective classroom management should be a concern, a primary concern. As a catechist, good will and an active faith life will not cover for a lack of effective classroom management skills. These skills are vital to your survival in the classroom setting, without them you can't hope to survive, much less to be successful. Your ministry as catechist requires that you be able to manage the four variables — teacher, learner, subject matter and learning environment — in a way which create a setting for your students' faith to become "living, conscious, and active, through the light of instruction." This is why classroom management is not only important but essential if you are to become an effective and successful catechist.

2
SETTING A DIRECTION

The Cat only grinned when it saw Alice. It looked good-natured, she thought: still it had very long claws and a great many teeth, so she felt it ought to be treated with respect.

"Cheshire-Puss," she began, rather timidly, as she did not at all know whether it would like the name: however, it only grinned a little wider. "Come, it's pleased so far," thought Alice, and she went on. "Would you tell me, please, which way I ought to go from here."

"That depends a good deal on where you want to get to," said the Cat.

"I don't much care where. . . ." said Alice.

"Then it doesn't matter which way you go," said the Cat.

" . . . so long as I get somewhere," Alice added as an explanation.

"Oh, you're sure to do that," said the Cat, "if you only walk long enough."

Lewis Carroll
Alice in Wonderland

Where Do I Begin?

The first step in becoming an effective classroom manager is to believe you can be one. You can. But in order to make this belief a reality you must know where you and your students are to end up at the end of the school year or semester. Thus, the second step in becoming an effective classroom manager is to know where you are going. If you don't, you will end up like Alice. You will find yourself, as a catechist, doing things, just for the sake of doing them and not because they are helping you and your students to reach your destination. To prevent this, you are *to know, to feel* and to be able *to do* as a result of their time with you in the classroom. If you don't have these goals clearly in mind, you, like Alice, will wander aimlessly. Why is this the case?

Teaching is an intentional activity. This means that teaching, by its very nature, tries to influence the behavior of students. Teacher and student come together in the classroom setting to learn "something." Parents enroll their children in parish catechetical programs because they want their children to learn "something." This "something" to be learned is the goal, and it must be clearly identified. It does no good to say, "Oh, they are supposed to learn about God." "What are they supposed to learn about God?" is the better question. The effective catechist knows the answer.

How are you to discover what your students are to learn? The best place to start is by looking at the textbook series you will be using. Almost every catechetical textbook series, approved by dioceses in the United States, provides an overview of the "something" that the students who use the series are supposed to learn. Later you will be asked to make a listing of the specified learning outcomes (those things that the student is expected to know, the attitudes to be developed, and the skills to be developed by year's end) for your grade level. But before you're asked to do this, let's talk about the textbook.

What Is A Textbook?

Student's Text

A good textbook serves four purposes for the student.

PRESENTER	EXPLICATOR
ILLUSTRATOR	TRAINER

(Lee C. Deighton in *The Encyclopedia of Education,* 1971)

First, it is a PRESENTER. The textbook communicates the subject matter which is considered important for a student, and it does so in a manner that is geared to the students' age and developmental readiness. Second, the textbook serves as an EXPLICATOR. It articulates the relationships that exist in the material it presents. Again, this explanation is according to the competence and maturity of the student. Third, the textbook functions as an ILLUSTRATOR for students by using graphics, charts, diagrams, photographs and drawings to illustrate these relationships. Fourth, the catechetical textbook functions as a TRAINER. It contains exercises, study questions and practice materials to develop the learners' religious lifestyle.

It is generally agreed that textbooks profoundly influence the learning environment. Religion textbooks are no different. They have their influence on how the learner views himself or herself; they provide a perspective on creation; and they begin the process of religious conceptualization. There is no doubt that religious understandings and attitudes can be and are influenced through textbooks. With this in mind, you should not take your students' textbook for granted. It is a valuable resource, and one that you will have to spend time with. However, there is a guide available, and it is called the "Teacher Manual."

Teacher Manual

In addition, to providing a textbook to serve as an EXPLAINER, PRESENTER, ILLUSTRATOR and TRAINER for students, catechetical textbook publishers also provide a grade level teacher manual which is each of these and more for you, the catechist. There are usually two editions of the teacher manual. One is for catechists who are teaching in a Catholic school setting where they may be teaching a religion class every day. The other is for you, the parish catechist who is teaching only once a week. Be sure you have the right edition. There is a difference. The parish religious education program edition is designed for use in a program that has classes scheduled once a week for approximately thirty weeks a year.

To be an effective classroom manager and a successful catechist, you must learn to use both the student textbook and the teacher manual to their full potential. However both books must be kept in perspective. They are invaluable resources. But that is all they are, resources. They are not the end all and be all of parish catechesis. Your task as catechist is to help your students' faith develop, not to assure that they know the textbook, except to the degree that the textbook helps their faith become "living, conscious and active." The textbook is an instructional tool. The teacher manual is a guide to using this tool effectively. The following is a process to guide you in becoming familiar with your teacher manual.

Get An Overview

A good teacher manual provides an introductory overview of the subject matter that is to be covered during the school year. The first thing you should do is read this section. Find out what is expected of both you and your students. As you are reading, ask yourself the following questions:

- Do I feel comfortable with the material?

- Do I agree with the approach being taken in the book?

- What are the strengths of the approach?

- What are the weaknesses?

- What do I have to learn in order to use the series effectively?

- Am I the right person to be using this series?

Asking questions like these will help you to not only know what you are to teach and how, but it will also help you to decide if in fact you are the right person to be teaching from this textbook series.

Be A Part Of The Team

If you find that you have a number of difficulties with the material or the manner in which it is to be taught, it may be that you should not be teaching on this level or perhaps you shouldn't be teaching at all. If there are problems, talk them over with your director of religious education. It will do neither you nor the program any good if you are teaching in a program that you don't agree with or if you feel you have to save the students from the program. If you have problems, deal with them outside of the classroom, through the channels that are available in the parish.

To be an effective catechist and ultimately a successful one, you have to like what you are doing. This means you need to be in agreement with the basic direction that is being taken in your parish program. If you are not, your frustration level will rise as the year goes on and neither you nor the students will be well-served. So carefully read the overview and make a decision. There is nothing wrong with saying you are not the person for the job. However, the hope is that in reading this section you will find yourself becoming more and more excited about the possibilities. If this happens, you're on your way.

Know What is Happening

Most teacher manuals provide a scope and sequence chart. This is an outline of what is designed to take place on each grade level in the program. It is the curriculum, the course to be followed in the series. It is important to study this chart so that you know where you and your students fit in the overall curriculum. Ask yourself what the focus of the various grade levels are, pre-school, fourth grade, seventh grade, eleventh grade. It is important that you know where your students have been and where they are going. Note such things as when the students should know certain prayers, when and what the students learn about the sacraments, how the series develops an understanding of the God of your tradition. Remember, textbooks have changed. They are different from when you were in school. Don't be too critical. Find out what is happening now. Ask yourself how you can become a part of the church's current approach to catechesis.

Get A Developmental Profile

If you have never taught, one of the most important sections in your teacher manual is that which provides a developmental profile of the students for whom the textbook is written. In this section you will find a description of the physical, emotional, intellectual, moral and religious assumptions the author(s) make about the students who will be using the text. These are the understandings that influenced the choice of activities, vocabulary, pictures, etc. used in the textbook. You will need to thoroughly understand these assumptions if you are to use the textbook effectively.

A careful reading of this section will not suffice. You should also spend some time discussing these assumptions with your director of religious education and the other catechists in the program, particularly those who have taught on your level. It is important to find out as much as you can about how children or young adults on your grade level behave. A key to maintaining a well-managed classroom is to know what to expect and what to ignore. If you have no understanding of where your students are developmentally, you are lost from the beginning.

A caution: don't count on your experience as a parent to make you a good catechist. Children are different in the classroom. The environment has its influence. You have probably heard of the parent, or been the parent, who exclaimed to a teacher or principal, "That's not my child you're describing!" That parent, or you, is right. It isn't the same child because you don't know your child in the classroom. We all behave differently in different settings. The classroom is a different setting. The skills required for handling children in peer groups are different from the skills needed for parenting. There are some very good parents who are poor catechists, just as there are some very good catechists who have a rough time as parent.

Make Your Mark

As you read the teacher manual, write down, highlight or underline those findings that are new to you or that you think are extremely important for you as a catechist. Mark only those things that are key for you. Remember, not everything is important for you. You need to read the teacher manual in light of who you are and what you need to know in order to be an effective and successful catechist. Make your notations in the manual itself. The teacher manual is your guide book, make it your own. Don't be afraid to write in it. You'll need to refer to it often in your early days of teaching, not just when you're conducting the class.

Keep Yourself Booked Up

Again, in addition to carefully reading what your teacher manual says about students, ask your DRE and the more experienced catechists to share their insights regarding the children or young adults in your parish. Most teacher manuals provide a bibliography. Select one or two books that are recommended in your manual or by your DRE or other catechists and make it a point to read them in the course of the year. A good teacher is always learning. If you have chosen to be a catechist, you have chosen to be a teacher. Be a good one. Read.

Use Parent Notes

Teacher manuals usually inform you about the use of parent notes if they are provided with the textbook series. Parent notes are provided as a resource to parents but they can also be an invaluable resource to the catechist. If you read these notes, not only will you know what the authors of your textbook would like to have the parents do as a follow-up from your class session or in preparation for the next lesson, but you also have a very clear statement about what the child should know, do, or feel as a result of their time with you in the classroom. In those settings where I have worked with catechists and we have taken the time to review the parent notes, it has added a great deal of insight and clarity into their lesson planning. Don't ignore the parent notes.

Know the Catechetical Process

Every textbook series has its own approach to lesson planning and development. This approach is called the catechetical process and is designed to normally take place within a sixty to ninety minute class session. This process usually has three steps.

Catechetical Process

Life Experience
↓
Development of Theme
↓
Application to Life

The process begins with some type of introduction which centers on a life experience as an introduction to the doctrinal content of the lesson. This normally takes twenty to twenty-five minutes of class time. For example, if the third grade lesson has as its theme forgiveness, it may begin with a real life story that deals with two children getting in a fight and one of the characters saying she or he is sorry. The children would read or act out the story and then enter into a discussion of the story with questions that are designed to center the children's attention on the theme.

This life experience movement is followed by activities designed to develop the doctrinal content of the lesson. The children might be presented with a saying of Jesus and how Jesus wants us to live together in peace and that this can only happen if we promise to forgive one another. The children might then recite the Our Father.

To conclude the lesson the children might be asked to indicate how they can be a forgiving person at home or among their friends. This activity would conclude the lesson by helping the children to apply the lesson to their life. Unless you clearly understand how lessons are developed and how you are to proceed in a class session, you will not effectively use your textbook. (But this need not happen and it won't if you are clear on the catechetical process employed in your textbook series.)

We once had a catechist come to us and say she was really disappointed with the program because there was no "religion" in any of the lessons. We asked what she meant, and she said that each week they would spend the whole class time doing some activity that the children seemed to enjoy, but they weren't learning anything about God. In our discussion, it became evident that she thought she could use either the introductory activity, the doctrinal development, or the concluding activity. She did not realize that each of these movements in the catechetical process was an essential part of one class session.

This example points to our failure as DREs to insure that this catechist understood the textbook series we were using in the parish. But it can serve as a good example to you as to how important it is that you clearly understand the catechetical process employed in your textbook series. A careful reading of your teacher manual provides this information. Take some time now to identify what the process is in your series. On a sheet of paper or in the boxes below list the movements of the catechetical process employed in your textbook. Some series have four or five movements.

Catechetical Process

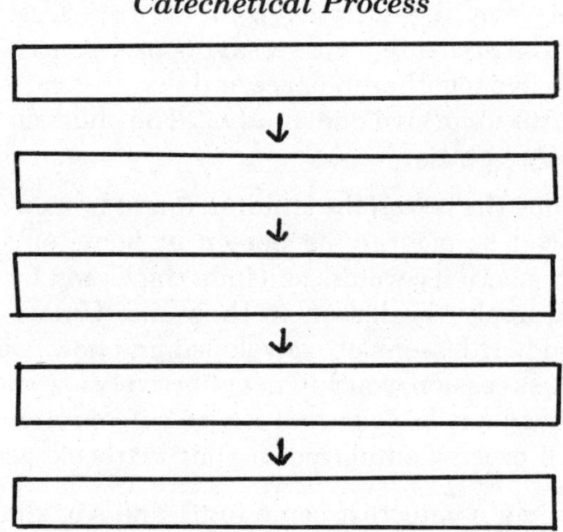

Be Flexible

Finally, with all of this talk about the value of the textbook series, don't forget that you are the catechist and the textbook, the teacher manual and the parent notes are only tools. They are aids to assist you in your ministry as a catechist. They are not ends in themselves. Don't be afraid to deviate from the text and to adapt it to your situation. You are not teaching a textbook series; you are teaching children and young adults. Your task is to insure that their faith is nourished, not that they learn the textbook. The textbook is of value only to the degree that it aids in this process.

In Conclusion

The successful catechist is effective. Effective catechists help their students' faith become "living, conscious, and active through the light of instruction." Your textbook series can be a valuable resource. It is a guide to where you are going and how you can get there. Use it. If you are new or uncertain as to what to do, carefully follow the guidelines provided in your teacher manual. In the beginning, you cannot err in faithfully following the book. It takes confidence to be an effective classroom manager. You can't have confidence if you don't know where you are going. The textbook series can help. It lets you know where you want to get to and which way you ought to go to get there.

3

CREATING A SPACE

A small child was drawing a picture and his teacher said, "That's an interesting picture. Tell me about it."

"It's a picture of God."

"Well nobody knows what God looks like."

"They will when I get done."

What Is A Classroom Supposed To Do?

Most parish programs use the space that is available for classrooms. Sometimes this is an old school building, the Catholic school in the evening, a multi-purpose room, or the rectory basement. Depending on the parish, classroom facilities range from poor to excellent. Finances often dictate what is available and possible and what is not. Catechists often have to be creative. The important thing for you as a beginner is to know what your classroom is like and what it will allow you to do and not to do. With this knowledge, you can realistically plan your lessons.

If you are to be an effective classroom manager, you need to design a classroom environment that is conducive to learning and is supportive of the catechetical process you will be using. You will need to create a place where both you and your students feel safe and secure. Your classroom is to be a place where faith can be nourished, understood and put into practice. It is to be a place where each student can draw his or her picture of God with the confidence and trust of the child spoken of above. To create this environment you must start with the physical design of the classroom you will be using. Classroom layout is a key variable in the teaching/learning process, and one over which you have some control.

Get A Feel For The Room

One of the first things you should do after offering your services as a catechist is to arrange to visit your classroom. This room is going to be the center of your catechetical activities. You should not even begin to read your teacher manual without some idea of what your classroom looks like physically. Walk around the room. How does it fit? What feelings do you have? Are they feelings of a happy learning environment? Do you get a closed in feeling? A feeling of freedom? Remember the feelings you have are not dissimilar to those your students will experience. Because the classroom is a key variable in the catechetical enterprise, you are going to have to work with this space when you are planning your lessons. After this initial visit you will be able to read your teacher manual and to adapt the lesson plans it provides to the classroom space you're going to be working in. You will also be able to make note of what you will have to do to the room to make it a place that contributes to the intent of a particular lesson.

Other things to make note of when you are in your room are:

- Are the desks moveable?

- Is there space to set up group activities or prayer areas?

- Is the room carpeted?

- Will the students be able to move easily from activity to activity?

- Can films or filmstrips be easily shown in the room?

• If it is a classroom that is used during the day for a regular school room, does it look like you will be able to personalize it for your class?

• Is there space for displaying the students' projects?

Reflect On Your Reactions

Do you find the classroom totally to your liking or one that you don't feel at all comfortable with? Your reaction should be made known to the DRE. If it is very negative, it may be a reaction that can be overcome (beginner's butterflies), or it may be a good reason for not teaching. To be an effective catechist you are going to have to use this space to its best advantage. To do this you need to take an honest look and rate your chances for success.

Current catechetical texts usually require space for large and small group activities, particularly on the lower elementary levels. Does the classroom you will be working in provide this type of space? If not, will you be able to adapt the suggested lesson plans to the space provided? Again on the lower elementary level, many textbook series suggest prayer corners and activity centers. Will you be able to provide these in your setting? If not, how will you adjust?

Draw A Floor Plan

If you have made up your mind to be a catechist, take the time to draw up an accurate floor plan of your classroom. Be sure to note all of the resources that are available — desks, windows, chalkboards, work areas, etc. (see the diagram). Your drawing will prove valuable in reading your teacher manual and in planning how to rearrange the room to best teach your lesson, and, if rearranging is impossible, how you will adapt your lesson planning to the space and resources available.

Sample Floor Plan

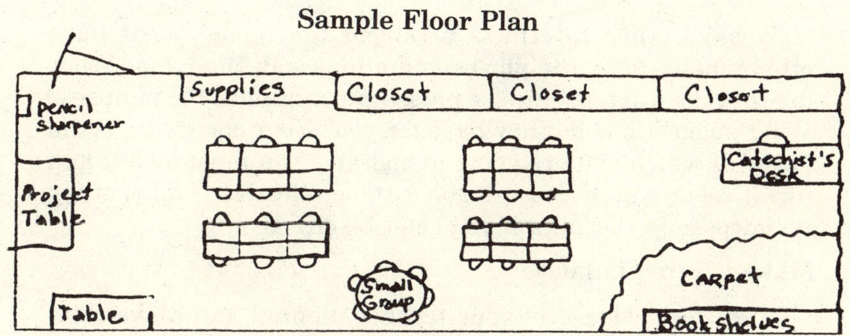

List The Pluses And The Minuses

Make a listing of all of the pluses that you see in your classroom. A plus is anything that you think will help you as a teacher and will facilitate the students' ability to learn. List as many things as possible. The longer your list the better. Now make a listing of the minuses, those things that you consider to be drawbacks. Answer the question, "How will this classroom interfere with my ability to teach effectively?" You are not being negative in doing this, only realistic. To use the classroom environment to its full potential, you need to know its strengths and weaknesses. Making these lists will help.

Talk It Over

After you've visited your classroom and compiled your lists, schedule a time to meet with your DRE and/or the other catechists who have used your room in the past. Bring your diagram of the classroom's strengths and weaknesses to the meeting. At this meeting learn as much as you can about how to use your classroom to its fullest potential. Listen carefully to what is said. Keep asking yourself, "How can I incorporate what is being said?" You will never have the perfect room, but you can create a space that will facilitate the students' learning and accentuate the gifts you bring as catechist.

Find out how much flexibility you have in designing or rearranging the room. Can you get extra tables? chairs? carpeting?

How have other catechists arranged the room? What have others found to be the pluses and minuses in the room? What did they do to accentuate the pluses and minimize the minuses? What suggestions do they have for you? Your classroom is the space in which you are going to operate. You must own it and use it creatively if you are going to be effective. And there is no purpose in teaching if you can't be effective.

Make It Functional

With a knowledge of your teacher manual and a sketch of your floor plan, you are ready to start designing the room according to your needs as a catechist. If you can design your classroom space in such a way that a positive answer can be given to the following questions, you will be well on your way to effectively using your room as an aid to classroom management.

> **Will all of the students be able to see me when I am addressing the class?**
> Spend some time determining where you are going to stand when you are addressing the class. Careful monitoring of students is a key to effective classroom management. You cannot do this if you cannot see the students or if they cannot see you. There must be clear lines of sight between you and the students when you are presenting materials or giving directions, as well as when you are sitting at your desk.
>
> **Are the high traffic areas free from congestion?**
> High traffic areas include work areas, prayer corners, book shelves, pencil sharpeners, students' desks and your desk. These areas, to the degree possible, should be separated from each other; there should be plenty of space to get to each area. This will prevent distractions and cut down on disciplinary problems.
>
> **Are student supplies readily accessible?**
> Ready access to materials allows activities to begin and to end on time with a minimum amount of con-

fusion. On the early elementary levels where most catechetical texts suggest activities that require the use of numerous supplies, it is important that you have the distribution of supplies well planned because of the limited amount of time that you have for each class session. If your textbook series places a heavy emphasis on activities, you should consider the use of aides — mothers, fathers, teenagers, and other parishioners who want to help in the program.

Can the students see the chalkboard and other displays?

To prevent classroom disruptions, all of the students should be able to see the chalkboard, overhead projector, movie screen, etc. without having to turn their desks around, or to sit in an uncomfortable position. If students cannot see or have to crane their necks, you are encouraging them not to pay attention to the presentation, and misbehavior is sure to follow. One distracted student is like a magnet. He or she attracts another student and before long the whole class is distracted; you have lost control.

If you can answer yes to the above questions, you have probably designed a functional classroom setting that promotes teaching and learning because it minimizes many of the common causes of student misbehavior.

Make The Classroom Visually Appealing

First impressions are important. When children enter your classroom, they should be entering a room that says this is an ordered environment in which I am going to be safe and can learn. This is accomplished by having all of the tables and chairs carefully arranged. At the start of the year, especially on the lower elementary levels, there should be at least the following displays for the walls and chalkboard:

- Class rules — these should be few in number (See Chapter 5)

- Some decorative display that captures the theme of the week's lesson

- A display that contains the names of all of the students in the class

You should cover bare bulletin boards with colored paper. You do not have to spend a lot of time decorating your room, but it should look cared for. Just as you clean and arrange your home when visitors are coming, so too, your classroom should visually say to your students that you knew they were coming and that you prepared for them.

Don't overdecorate. Cluttered walls and bulletin boards make the classroom look more like a play room than a place for learning. An overly decorated room will be a source of distraction to the students. Visually your room should say, "This is a well-ordered and pleasant place in which to learn."

Make The Room a Teaching Tool

Because students come together so seldom in parish programs, your classroom can be used as a reminder of what was covered in previous sessions. Use the bulletin boards to display student papers or projects. Refer to these at the beginning of the class session as a review of the previous weeks' activities.

You can also use bulletin boards or walls to display key words, prayers, or symbols that you want the students to know or to be familiar with. Refer to these aids as you teach. By using the classroom itself as a teaching tool, the students come to associate the room itself with learning.

Keep The Room In Good Repair

Many parish programs have limited resources. However, those resources that are available should be in working order. As a new catechist the time spent examining each desk, making sure there is a desk for each child, checking the light switches, seeing if there are enough hooks for each child to hang his or her coat on, testing the chalkboards to be sure they can be written on and erased (there are some that cannot), is time well spent. Many a new catechist has lost control of a class on the first day because there weren't enough desks, a child got a desk that tilted and distracted the whole group, or he or she went to the chalkboard to write and couldn't. Control that is lost in the first class is never regained.

Even though it is the DRE's responsibility to see to it that these things are taken care of, you will do well to check for yourself. Better safe than sorry.

Have A Place For Everything And Everything In Its Place

A well-managed classroom is one that leaves very little to chance. Both you and the students should know where things are. It does little to promote an ordered learning environment if you are not able to find a pencil when one is needed, or if you need an extra textbook and can't find one. You would do well to spend some time figuring out where you will keep things in the classroom. Frequently used materials like glue, pencils, scissors, crayons, markers, etc., should be kept in a readily accessible place. You might even consider making your own supply boxes. Clearly mark the contents of each box.

In addition to supplies, students should know where they are to hang their coats, pick up their books, put their completed projects, etc. If you are new to teaching, you cannot overplan these details. A well-managed classroom is in part the result of a well-organized teacher. You will feel more in control if, in fact, you know where things are and know you can deal with most practical questions that are sure to arise.

Create Your Own Space

With these guidelines in mind and with the information and suggestions you've received from your DRE and other catechists, on a piece of paper or in the space below design a floor plan for your classroom. To begin, determine where you will conduct whole-class instruction. Even if there is very little that you can do with your setting, it is worthwhile to draw a floor plan. It will make the classroom setting more vivid in your mind and make it easier to visualize a class session when you are preparing your lessons.

My Classroom Layout

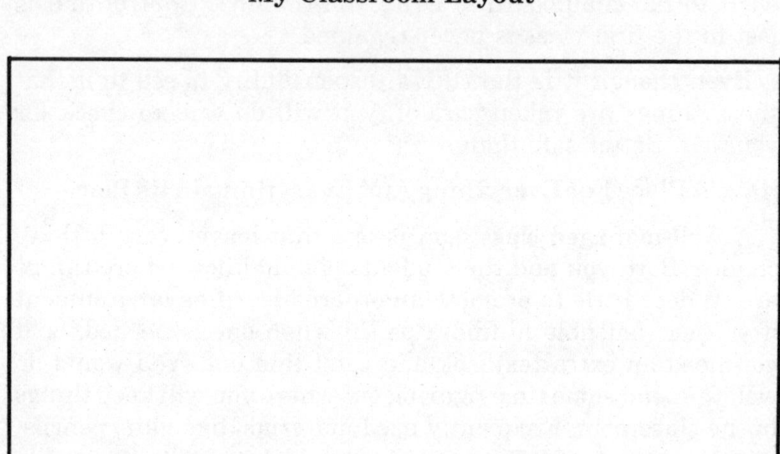

Review your layout. Can all of the children see you without a lot of movement? If you set up a small group area for prayer or reading and you will be in that area, can you see the whole group from your position in the group? Is your desk in a functional place? Are supplies and bookshelves easily reached? Is there enough space for students to hang up their coats?

In Conclusion

Don't ignore a serious evaluation of the classroom you'll be teaching in. Time spent with your DRE and other catechists discussing ways in which the classroom can be better utilized, is time well spent. How you use the classroom affects your success as a catechist. Successful catechists spend time to learn how to use their classroom creatively and effectively.

4
TEACHING A STUDENT

The secret of education lies in respecting the pupil.

Ralph Waldo Emerson

You see, really and truly, apart from the things any-
one can pick up (the dressing and the proper way of
speaking, and so on), the difference between a lady
and a flower girl is not how she behaves, but how
she's treated. I shall always be a flower girl to Profes-
sor Higgins, because he always treats me as a flower
girl, and always will; but I know I can be a lady to
you, because you always treat me as a lady, and al-
ways will.

Eliza Doolittle to Colonel Pickering
in George Bernard Shaw's *Pygmalion*

What Is A Student?

This probably strikes you as a strange question in light of
the two quotes above. A student isn't a "What." Each student
is a unique individual. But as a catechist you are responsible
for working with unique individuals in their peer group. You
are to relate to unique individuals in their role as student and
from your role as catechist. And just as you had to answer the
question, "What Is A Catechist?" in order to clarify your role,

so too, you must have an accurate image of what a student is if you plan to be an effective catechist.

The students you are responsible for are the children of the members of you parish community; some may even be the children of your close friends and neighbors. They are people you know personally. But this relationship will change when you enter the classroom. You will no longer be relating to these children as Mrs. or Mr. Jones the friend and neighbor. In the classroom you become Mrs. or Mr. Jones the catechist, the "teacher." You have a role to fulfill. This role makes your relationship different.

The children, for their part, come to you not as the sons and daughters of your friends and neighbors, but as learners. Your friendship or "neighborness" is fine, but it is not the reason for your coming together in the classroom. You and the children come together to formally engage in instructional activities that are designed to make their faith become "living, conscious and active." They are children enrolled in a parish catechetical program. The children come to you as students.

Student is the name applied to each child or young adult in your classroom. He or she is in your classroom to discover a new or better way of relating to the world. As a result of participating in your planned classroom activities, the student should know, feel and be able to do things he or she did not know, or feel or was incapable of doing before the class. Or if the student already knew, felt or had certain skills when he or she entered the classroom, the knowledge should be broadened, the attitudes challenged and developed, and the skills noticeably perfected.

How Can I Do All Of This?

To begin with you need some ways of viewing a student that are helpful for teaching. These perspectives must accurately image the student both as a person and as a learner. The following suggestions are based on generally accepted explanations of the person and of personal learning styles.

Focus On The Whole Person

One perspective that we have found helpful and which informs many of today's textbook writers is the view from educational psychology that each student is a THINKING, FEELING, and ACTING person.

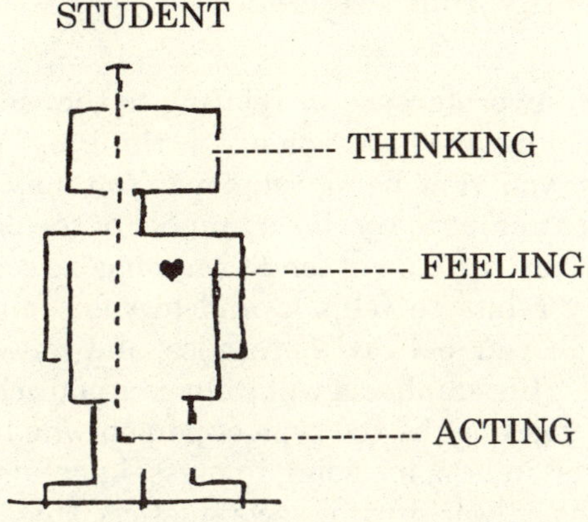

Using this model, your students, as thinking persons, need to arrange their world intellectually — they need to be helped to name their experience. To teach that our God is called Father is to help the student think about (to name) the God of our tradition. However, as this model shows, individuals do not relate to the world simply as thinking persons. They also feel things. Feelings influence almost everything that we do. To help your students get in touch with their feelings about a person from another racial or ethnic grouping and to allow them to challenge their feelings in light of the Christian story is to teach for a change in attitude. Finally, individuals act. They do things. As a catechist, if you teach a child to make the Sign of the Cross, to find a passage in the Scriptures, or to provide comfort to the elderly, you have taught him or her how to act. You have developed a skill.

This is a helpful way to view the learner. If you are to be an effective catechist, you must teach the whole person — thinking, feeling and acting. The ability to do this will take time because we all tend to live our lives predominantly out of one of these dimensions. Each of your students tends to relate to the world predominantly out of one of these dimensions, just as you do.

Identify Your Preference

Your preference in relating to the world will influence your teaching. Perhaps you are a "thinking" person. This will affect how you view being religious. You may conceive of religion as the attempt to resolve a number of theological questions. When you teach, you will tend to emphasize cognitive content. Or you may relate to religion and to your faith life on the "feeling" level. You feel God's presence, and you want to share this feeling. This emphasis will influence your choice of class activities. Or you may be the type of person who believes religion is captured in actions, going to mass, kneeling in prayer, feeding the hungry, working for social justice. This, too, will affect the way you teach.

Being religious cannot be limited to knowing a content or having a feeling or performing particular activities. It is a combination of all of these. And a good catechist will attempt to develop each of these dimensions of personality in his or her students over the course of a year. Realize that every student has a preference that must be respected and utilized because it will influence how he or she behaves in the classroom. To help you clarify your preference, spend some time reflecting on which dimension — thinking, feeling or acting, tends to predominate in your life. On a sheet of paper or in the space provided below, complete these two sentences: "I tend to live my life predominately out of the ___(Thinking, Feeling, Acting)___ dimension." "This is reflected in my religious life in the following ways ."

> I tend to live my life predominately out of the ___________ dimen-sion. This is reflected in my religious life in the following ways. . . .

Respect Learning Styles

Students who enter your classroom, besides having a prefer-ence for the thinking, feeling and acting dimension of their personality, also come with individual learning styles. Not everyone learns in the same way. Researchers identify three basic learning styles — visual (seeing), oral (spoken), and phys-ical (doing).

Learning Styles

visual
oral
physical

Again the best way to understand these learning styles is to see how they apply in your life. Do you learn best by seeing things in print or graphically illustrated? If so, you may be a visual learner. Are you a person who learns best by listening? You are an oral learner. Or perhaps, you learn best through 'hands on' experience, by doing things. If this is the case, physical learning may be your predominant style. Of course, we use all three of these learning styles and some activities lend themselves more easily to one style than to another. Making a clay pot is best learned by making a clay pot. However, when you were in a classroom, which did you find most helpful? Did you prefer to read? To listen to a lecture? To work in the lab? Your preference will probably carry over into your teaching.

If you learn best through illustrations, you will probably teach by using illustrations. If you find lectures the most appealing way to learn, you will no doubt emphasize the formal presentation in your lesson. And if you are a "roll up your sleeves" and "let's do it" type of person, this will probably be reflected in your classroom style. This is okay. In fact, if you can't bring your learning style to bear on your teaching, you will probably be ineffective and frustrated. If you are a doing person, you will find yourself at your wits end if the catechetical program requires that you only lecture. Likewise, if you are a marvelous story teller and you are allowed only to let the students engage in activities and share their perceptions and feelings, you'll no doubt have a rough time. Your learning style needs to be built upon, not ignored or squelched.

Identify Each Student's Learning Style

As soon as possible, find out which students like to read (visual learners), which students enjoy class presentations, or listening to stories (oral learners), and which students enjoy projects and other types of activities (physical learners). Do you have a large number of students who favor a particular style? Realizing that every style is going to be represented in your room, you should know if there is a particular style that predominates in the class. This knowledge can guide your selection of the suggested class activities in your teacher manual.

Your students have their own preferences for asking and answering religious questions and for living their religious lives. If you are going to touch each student at some point in the course of the semester or school year, you will have to appeal to his or her particular emphasis. His or her emphasis may not be yours. This is why it is important to maintain a balance in your lesson planning. A disservice is rendered to the student who wants to know about prayer but is only provided with experiences of praying. Likewise, the seventh graders who want to do something for the poor will be frustrated if all of the classes only talk about the problem of poverty. Try to get some sense of each student's learning style.

Rely On Your Teacher Manual

The most practical answer to the question of how to focus on each of these dimensions of personality and the various learning styles is to follow the lesson plans suggested in your teacher manual. If you are using a diocesan approved textbook, it is probably written from this three-fold conceptualization of the person and suggests a variety of learning activities that will appeal to the various learning styles described. Your task is to make the right decisions to create a blend of activities that meets both the personal and the learning style needs of each student in your class.

5
TEACHING STUDENTS

> *Meanwhile it is enough to point out that there are many more pupils than teachers in the world, so that the average teacher must spend several hours a day with a collection of ten to thirty youngsters. Unless he (sic) likes groups of young people, he will not teach them well. It will be useless to wish that there were only two or three, or that they were all more mature. They will always be young, and there will always be lots of them.*

> Gilbert Highet
> *The Art of Teaching*

Student or Students, What's The Difference?

In the previous chapter we focused on the individual student. We emphasized that all students are alike in that they can think, feel and act. At the same time we showed that each student is unique and tends to have a predominant learning style. The teacher's challenge is to respect the individuality of learning styles in a classroom full of students. This is also the challenge of the classroom catechist. You are responsible for helping the faith of an individual student become living, conscious and active in a room full of students who are all different. This is the skill, the gift, that you must develop, the ability to design and implement learning activities that nurture the faith of each student individually while appealing to the larger group. The lessons presented in your teacher manual are suggested ways of doing this.

It is much easier to help a student ask his or her religious questions and seek answers on a one to one basis than it is in a group. The classroom changes how the questions must be asked and how the answers will be sought. But there is something to be gained in this setting. It is an opportunity for the student to interact with his or her peers in learning about the religious community in which he or she is growing up. There is value in hearing how your age-mates think and feel. It can be both affirming and challenging provided the classroom where the interaction takes place is a safe and secure place for learning. Not all classrooms are. Yours can be.

The following guidelines will help you manage your classroom in a way that will permit you to carry out your lesson plan and to insure that each student is respected and has an opportunity to learn.

Learn Names

Initially, nothing is more effective in helping a student feel that he or she belongs than that you know his or her name. Also, calling a student by name is one of the quickest ways to prevent a classroom disruption. Every student has a name. Learn it. Rehearse the pronunciation of each name. If you are stumped on a particular name, find someone who knows how to pronounce it. Use name tags until you can call each student by name. On the upper levels, let the students know that you are using name tags so that you can get to know them. They will complain, but that's okay. They appreciate the effort.

Know Something Special About Each Student

Many textbook series provide an introductory lesson that is designed to have each student say what is special about him or her. Use this activity. Jot down what each student says about himself or herself. Refer to these unique characteristics throughout the year when you are conducting class. To say something like, "Jennifer, remember when you said you liked to draw. Well, in this lesson we are. . . ." A reference like this builds a sense of belonging in Jennifer, and it lets the group know that each member of the class is important. It lets the class know that you listen to their comments and that you think what they have to say is important. The use of such references builds continuity with earlier classes; this is important in a program where you are meeting with the students only once a week.

Identify Students Who Need Special Attention

Find out if you have any children with learning disabilities, physical handicaps, allergies, etc. Do you have any exceptionally talented children? They will require special attention if they are not to be bored. A bored student is a potential behavior problem. Which students are well-liked? Disliked? Play to each student's strengths. Because you are not a professional teacher and have a limited amount of time with the students, you will not be able to concern yourself with remedial activities.

Because students come with varying reading skills, don't design or choose lessons that require that each child take a turn reading aloud. Have good readers read. Call on students to do those things that they do well. Each student is good at something, even if it is passing out books or sharpening pencils. Identify these skills and use them in the catechetical process.

Be Directive

When students walk into your room, in their minds it's just another classroom. You are in direct competition with every other teacher they have had and every other classroom they've entered. They don't care that this is a religion class. A classroom is a classroom when you are a student. It is essential for your success as a catechist and their success as learners that you and your room compare favorably with the better teachers and classrooms they've experienced. This can only happen if you are confident and in control. This does not mean you have to be authoritarian. Rather, you must exude confidence because you know what is to happen and how it is to happen. Students need to know that someone is in control. That someone is you.

State Your Expectations

A safe and secure classroom is a predictable one. Students should know what is supposed to happen and how it is to happen. This is best accomplished by having a set of classroom procedures. The classroom procedures should be clearly stated, known by the students, and consistently enforced. This frees the student from worrying about what he or she should do or not do and allows him or her to focus on the task at hand.

The following are suggested procedures for first grade through third grade and for fourth grade through eighth grade classrooms.

Sample Classroom Procedures, First Grade To Third Grade

1. We go to our seats when we enter the room.
2. We listen to the teacher.
3. We raise our hand if we want to talk.
4. We help keep the room neat.
5. We take turns. We help each other.
6. We are quiet so everyone can hear.

Sample Classroom Procedures, Fourth Grade to Eighth Grade

1. Bring your textbook to class.

2. Go to your seat when you enter the room and talk quietly until class begins.

3. Contribute to class discussions.

4. Raise your hand and wait to be recognized to talk.

5. Respect the opinions of others.

6. Protect desks, school supplies, and other equipment.

7. Wait to be dismissed by the teacher.

Use the above procedures as a guide for establishing your own. It would be valuable to discuss classroom procedures with your DRE and with the other catechists who teach or who have taught on your grade level. It is good if all catechists on a grade level agree on the same procedures. Remember rules should be kept to a minimum, and they should be the essential elements for maintaining a safe and secure learning environment. These procedures should be explained in the first class session and referred to when necessary. Display them in the classroom. Keep rules to a minimum, and be sure they apply to everyone.

Focus On The Behavior Not The Student

If a student should fail to observe a classroom procedure and needs to be corrected, focus your comments on the behavior not the student. It is better to say, "Johnny, when you want to talk remember to raise your hand." Rather than, "Johnny, don't you know the rules? You never pay attention. Raise your hand if you have something to say." In the first example you are criticizing Johnny's failure to raise his hand before speaking. In the second you are criticizing Johnny. It is the behavior, not Johnny, that is the problem.

Affirm Each Student Individually

Take the time before and after class to talk to your students. Arrive early for class and stay an extra few minutes after. Simple comments like, "Sally, I saw your basketball game last night and you played well," or "Billy you look like you're ready for class today," go a long way in making the students feel wanted. In addition, affirming statements like these encourage students to want to do well in class. So much of learning is motivational. If students know that you care for them, they are more likely to be motivated to perform for you.

This type of personal motivation is particularly important in the catechetical classroom. Classroom education is dependent on some type of reward system, either internal or external. Students work to achieve something. It may be, in the best of cases, the thrill of learning or, more often than not, to achieve a passing grade. It is difficult for many students (particularly fourth grade and up) to develop a strong internal desire to come to religion class. As a result, students are not easily engaged in class activities. Internally, the subject is not that exciting, and there are not real external rewards or punishments to motivate. Grades are not generally given, or, if they are, they do not carry the same weight they carry in the regular school setting. Thus, student affirmation is a very important and effective tool in parish catechetical programs and should be used generously.

Keep Expectations High

Never speak down to your students. You should always address them in a way that is both affirming and challenging. "Suzie, you did a nice job retelling the story of the forgiving father. Let me add just a few details to the story . . . Class, do you think the father should have forgiven his son so easily?

Why?" is much better than "Suzie, you left out the most important part. Let me tell you what this story means."

In the first example you are affirming of Suzie's effort, you are able to respectfully correct any inaccuracies or add elements of the story that were left out, and you are engaging the class in a critical reflection on the story. In the second example, you are critical of Suzie's effort, and you make the assumption that the story cannot be interpreted by the students. The first approach creates a sense of involvement and challenge, the second is very passive and "boring."

Don't underestimate your students. Allow them freedom within bounds to become actively involved in the learning process. If students are not engaged, they become restless, and restless students are potential behavior problems. Keep your classes challenging by choosing or designing lesson plans that encourage the students to go a little bit further than they think they can.

4. Be Honest

Don't deceive students. If you don't have an answer say so. But be careful how you say it. You don't want to give the impression that you are unprepared or unqualified to be a catechist. Students are quick to make judgments about teachers, and it is difficult to change their minds once they are made up.

As catechist, you are the resource person in the class. So in responding to a question that you don't know the answer to, have the student restate the question for you and then indicate that you will provide an answer or a way to find the answer in the next class. If possible, offer some suggestions to the student as to what he or she might do during the week to come up with his or her own answer. In this way you are being honest, while retaining your role as catechist.

I am not intimating here that the catechist is to project the image of an answer person. What I am saying is that you can be effective in your role as catechist only if the students respect you. Respect for a classroom catechist, especially in the upper elementary grades, has a lot to do with the students' impression that the catechist is a well organized and knowledgeable teacher.

Keep It Confidential

Don't talk about students outside of class. This will be difficult at times because you know many of the students and their families from your involvement in the parish or the community. And depending on how you relate to a particular family, especially if you don't get along, there is going to be a tendency to say things like, "Oh, that Smith boy is just like his mother. No wonder he doesn't. . . ." The temptation is even worse if the child is a behavior problem. Don't give in. What happens in your classroom should stay in your classroom. Don't gossip.

There are times when you may have to talk about the Smith boy's behavior but this should be with the DRE or a catechist who can help you work with him to improve his behavior or to help you to improve your classroom management skills so that he won't need to misbehave. But at no time should this information be shared with your neighbor or others who have no need or right to know. Some students are surprisingly frank and open in what they say to a teacher. There is a confidentiality that goes with teaching. Observe it. Without this confidentiality, your classroom will never be a safe and secure place for learning.

In Conclusion

If you are going to be successful as a catechist in the classroom, you have to like working with groups. To work with students and at the same time help the individual's faith to become "living, conscious, and active," requires special skills. The guidelines provided in this chapter will help you to develop the basic skills. Your classroom can be a place where the children in your parish community can interact with their peers in such a way that their maturing faith is both nourished and challenged. Enjoy your group of students!

6

BECOMING A CLASSROOM TEACHER

First say to yourself what you would be; and then do what you have to do.

Epictitus
Discourses

What Do Successful Classroom Teachers Do?

You have chosen to be a catechist. You are now a part of the Church's catechetical ministry. You are a teacher. You have a vocation, a calling. You are called to echo the word of God in a special way. You are to do this not as a parent, though you may be one; not as a librarian, though you may be that too; nor as a banker, secretary, coach, whatever. You are to do it as a classroom teacher in your parish program. This is "what you would be." Now you must "do what you have to do."

What you have to do is develop the ability to think and to act like a classroom teacher. The suggestions that follow are taken from research on successful classroom teachers. They are their "tricks of the trade," the skills that they bring to their vocation as teacher. There is nothing mysterious in any of them. In fact, with self control and persistence you can develop each of them.

Think Positively

A positive self-image is essential to success in any endeavor. Whether you realize it or not, all of your actions, feelings and behavior are consistent with your conception of yourself. And you can control your self-image. If you think of yourself as a poor teacher, there is little that can be done to make you a good one. If you think you can't succeed, you won't. So if you want to be a successful catechist, affirm yourself. Whatever kind of person you would like to be or whatever changes you would like to make, the change has to come from within. So begin today to think of yourself as a successful teacher.

You must think of yourself as competent and able. It is important that you fill your head with positive images of yourself as teacher. What good does it do to tell yourself that you can't do it, that you can't be a successful teacher, that you can't control a room full of children? You can. Or at least there is a good chance that you can. But this will never happen if you're not convinced. So much of teaching is confidence. A poor self-image will not produce confidence. And a lack of confidence militates against your becoming an effective classroom manager.

To become a successful teacher, you have to believe it is possible. Associate with good teachers. Tell yourself things like the following: I can read the teacher manual and implement the lesson plan. I like being a teacher. I am good with children in a classroom. I'm looking forward to teaching this class. I ask good questions. I enjoy preparing for class. Fill your head with positive images. Don't let negative thoughts predominate. If you want to be a successful teacher, you can be one. Take your cues from those people you know who are good and effective teachers. Model their behavior. Think and act positively. You have everything to gain.

Plan Ahead

Effective teachers are always thinking about teaching. They are always planning their next lesson. Lesson planning is not limited to an hour or two the night before class. It is a way of life. Effective teachers do both formal and informal lesson planning. If you want to be an effective classroom manager, you need to train yourself to do both.

Formal Planning

Formal planning takes place when you sit down with the intention of preparing your lesson. You should try to schedule two formal planning sessions for each week's class. Schedule the first session as far in advance of the class as possible. At this first session, read through the coming week's lesson in your teacher manual. Familiarize yourself with the theology informing the lesson, the learning outcomes for the lesson, the class activities, the materials that will be needed, etc. By doing this you are giving yourself time to own the lesson and to deal with any difficulties you may have, be they theological, "What are they saying about sin?", or practical, "Where will I ever find 30 shoe boxes?"

If you are new, it would be good to schedule this first session at a time when either your DRE, the catechists who teach on your grade level, or someone who has had experience teaching in the parish program can be present. This is a much richer way to prepare for class. The company of others will alleviate many of the fears that you will naturally have. It can also provide you with more insights, both theological and practical, into the lesson plan. By scheduling your first formal planning session, either alone or with others, far in advance of class, you allow yourself the time you need for informal planning.

Informal Planning

Informal planning is essential to successful teaching. It is during this time that the lesson starts to come together and becomes your own. It is the time when you let the ideas from your formal planning session kick around in your head. Informal planning can take place when you are driving to work, cleaning a cupboard, scolding the dog, watching television, or changing a diaper. During these times you should be asking yourself questions like: Will the lesson plan work? How can I change it to fit my class? Which activity do I like best? It is during the informal planning period that many catechists discover how the theology that informs the lesson is actually reflected in the lesson plan. Informal planning must become a natural process for you. For it to be productive, it should be preceded by the first formal planning session described above.

The day before class set aside some time for your second formal planning session. This session should be done alone. Write out or review what you are going to do in class. Go through your lesson plan step by step. Make any changes that may have occurred to you during the week. At the end of this session, the lesson plan should be yours. Write it out (See Chapter 7). Check to see that you have all of the supplies. Is there anything else you will need? Get all of your supplies together. You don't want to be flying out the door for class the next day, hoping that you have everything you need. If that becomes your approach, there is little hope for your becoming an effective classroom manager and even less of your being a successful teacher. Better to plan ahead. You can do it. And it's fun.

Visualize

Once your lesson plan is written and you know what is to happen in class, sit back, close your eyes and picture vividly how the class will proceed. Picture yourself arriving early and greeting the students as they enter the classroom. What will you say to each student? Greet each student. Now start the class. Where will you stand? Picture yourself addressing the class. Use the words you plan on using. One of the children asks a question, how do you answer?

You should rehearse everything that you expect to take place in the classroom. Distribute supplies. Move from activity to activity. Explain a procedure. Collect the projects. Rehearsal will increase your confidence. It can also prevent your worrying about what you will do when you enter the room, because you've already done it. This exercise helps you to be a better classroom manager because it allows you to develop options. You feel prepared because you've tried to deal with every conceivable situation.

Focus On Learning Not Teaching

Effective teachers always think in terms of what the student will be able to do and then plan accordingly. Teaching is for learning. Train yourself to think first about what the student is supposed to learn and what behaviors will indicate to you that he or she has learned it. It is only after you have specified what the student will be able to do as a result of his or her participation in the class session that you are ready for the question, "What do I have to do as teacher?"

In specifying what the student should do, use action verbs. These are verbs that describe how you are going to know if learning took place. If the general objective is that the students will learn to pray, you need to specify the behaviors of the student that will indicate that this has happened. For example, the students will be able to *recite* the Hail Mary, *compose* their own prayer of thanksgiving, *read* the prayer of St. Francis. *Recite, compose,* and *read* are action verbs that specify what it means "to learn to pray" in your class session.

Many of today's teacher manuals do this for you. But you must learn to be conscious of these specific outcomes and to focus on them in your planning. By doing this you are focusing on the students and what they are to do. Your emphasis is on learning outcomes. The following list is a sampling of action verbs which will help you in the task of identifying and specifying learning outcomes.

Action Verbs for Stating General Learning Outcomes

Analyze	*Create*	*Interpret*	*Locate*	*Think*
Apply	*Demonstrate*	*Know*	*Recognize*	*Understand*
Appreciate	*Evaluate*	*Listen*	*Speak*	*Use*

Action Verbs for Stating Specific Learning Outcomes

Accept	Complete	Find	List	Perform
Agree	Contribute	Finish	Locate	Plan
Allow	Cooperate	Forgive	Make	Prove
Analyze	Color	Help	Move	Recite
Answer	Dance	Indicate	Name	Say
Argue	Disagree	Illustrate	Organize	Tell
Choose	Discuss	Join	Outline	Use
Communicate	Draw	Keep	Participate	Write

*(Adapted from Stating Objectives for Classroom Instruction
by Norman E. Gronland, 1978)*

You should always be able to state in action verbs what your students will do in your class as well as what they are to have learned from your class. The inability or the lack of willingness to do this has been and still is a problem in many parish catechetical programs. If you don't know what you want to do or if you are unclear about what you want to do, why do you invite the students to the class and how will you ever judge whether or not your teaching was effective?

Teaching is for learning. Develop the ability to clearly identify and state the learning outcomes you expect in your students; you will be a better teacher. Effective classroom teachers know what they want to do, how to do it, and if they've been successful.

Be Enthusiastic

Enthusiasm is catching. Successful teachers have the ability to create in their students an excitement and enthusiasm for the topic being studied. You can do this only if you see the importance in what you are doing, and if you enjoy what you are doing. To do this you need to know the material you are teaching. This can be accomplished by studying your teacher manual.

Enjoyment comes from bringing your own personality to the classroom. You are different. You are a unique catechist among all the other catechists in your parish program. Own your uniqueness and use it to your advantage. You can only really enjoy teaching when you realize that it is you who is teaching. You don't have to be someone else or someone else's expectation. You are in the classroom doing the best you can, and learning with every move. Enjoy it. If you do, the students will.

Learn to Laugh

Successful teachers have learned to laugh. Teaching is a serious activity, but not so serious that it isn't funny. If you can't laugh, you're not going to make it as a teacher, and for the student's sake shouldn't. The realization that the world is at best unpredictable and that your classroom is no different will help keep things in perspective. Murphy's law, "If something can go wrong, it will," should be engraved on your teacher manual. This isn't to say you shouldn't plan, just expect the unexpected and learn to smile. A successful teacher is flexible. To remain flexible in the classroom, one needs to keep in shape by developing a sense of humor.

There is only so much you can do in a classroom. It is not the center of a student's religious life, nor should it be. It is one hour a week, where a student under your guidance can learn about his or her religious tradition in the company of peers. It is not everything the student needs. It is not intended to be. Yet, it is important and it can and should be done well. But keep it in perspective. And when things don't work out as planned bring on the smile. Learn to laugh.

In Conclusion

Successful classroom teachers think well of themselves and enjoy teaching. They carefully plan their lessons and enter the classroom with an infectious enthusiasm. Model yourself on their behavior. Teaching is in part a skill, and skills can be learned. By thinking positively, planning ahead, visualizing your class sessions, focusing on learning outcomes, being enthused and learning to laugh, you will be modelling some of the skills that are common to successful classroom teachers. Every teacher who is considered a success will tell you that they still have their rough days and that there were many discouraging moments along the way. But the reward is worth it, seeing a child grow.

If you are to be successful as a classroom catechist, you need the same teaching skills as the successful classroom teacher. Teaching in a classroom setting is not easy, particularly if you are new. But you can do it. And the results, while not always immediate, are gratifying. You are helping the young on their religious journey. Do what you have to do to be the success that you know you can be!

7
PREPARING A LESSON

If you are always taught to do things the same way,
you learn only one way of doing things,
and it becomes harder to cope with all the new things
you'll have to face later on.

To learn anything useful it's important that you
should want to;
that you find the subject interesting;
that you understand why you have to learn it;
that you get a chance to say something yourself;
that you are allowed to work on the subject in your
own way;
that you are allowed to cooperate with your friends.

the little red schoolbook

What Is Lesson Planning?

The authors of *the little red schoolbook* advise students that if they are to learn they must want to learn. And as they continue, students will want to learn if they find the subject interesting, know why they are learning it and become involved in it both personally and communally with their friends. This advice to the student is also good advice for you as you plan your lessons.

Lesson planning is the teacher's homework. It is what a teacher has to do to come into the classroom prepared. As a classroom catechist, lesson planning must become a part of your weekly routine. In the last chapter we spoke of your need to set aside two formal lesson planning sessions for each class. During this time you plan what the student is to learn in class and how you will facilitate learning. There are two types of lesson planning: long range and immediate. Both types of planning have been started for you in your teacher manual. Your task is to adapt the manual's planning to your situation.

Long Range Planning

Long range lesson planning answers two questions, "What are we going to study this year?" and "When?" A general answer to the first question is often found in the title of the student's textbook; for example, *God, Our Father, We Celebrate the Eucharist, We Receive the Spirit of Jesus, Sacraments*. A more specific answer to this question is found by reading the lesson plans in your teacher manual.

The second question, "When?" is answered by relating the number of lessons in each unit of your textbook to the number of class sessions for the year. The text may provide 30 lessons, but you may meet the students only 20 times during the year. This type of planning should be done with the DRE and with the other catechists on your grade level. Together you can decide which of the suggested lessons should be used, which should be omitted and which seasonal lessons (Advent, Christmas, Lent, Easter) should be built into the year's plan.

Be conscious of time limits. If your parish program is like most catechetical programs, you will probably meet with the learners for an hour, twenty-five to thirty times in the course of the year. This is not much time. Often it is less time than the students spend in front of a television in one week! You must ask yourself what can you realistically do in this limited amount of time.

So before the school year begins, specify what it is that you intend for all of the students to learn by year's end. Doing this will put you in a better position to plan your individual class sessions because you know where you want to end up.

It is important that you prepare a long range plan. You need to know not only where you begin and where you end, but how you are to move from start to finish. If you don't know, you won't be able to put things into perspective. You will teach each class with no real knowledge of what's coming next. This makes it difficult for you to answer a question now or wait because it will be covered later. Without an overall plan clearly in mind, you may get all involved in answering a question that is given a whole class session the following week. If this happens often, your class will lose its focus, and you will lose control. To be an effective classroom manager, you need to be very clear on the purpose and direction of the class. You need to know when, where, and how things are going to happen.

Immediate Planning

Immediate lesson planning is your preparation of a class session. The process to be followed was described in the previous chapter. You remember that we talked about both the informal and formal preparation. Your teacher manual is the key resource for immediate planning (Review Chapter Two). Every good lesson has a beginning, middle and end. This process is captured in your textbook's catechetical plan. The following principles can serve as guides in matching the lesson plans in your teacher manual to your classroom setting.

Work To The Clock

Know how much time you have scheduled for your class session. This time-span is the framework from which you should read the suggested lesson plan. As you are reading the teacher manual or driving along thinking about the class, ask yourself, "How much time will I need for this?" Make a note. You should allot a specific amount of time for every planned activity. The following is an example of how a sixty minute class session can be broken down.

CLASS OUTLINE

Welcome students. Review last week's class. (5 min.)

Distribute activity sheets and explain how to use them. (5 min.)

Divide the class into groups of three and have the students complete activity sheets. (15 min.)

Conclude this activity by leading a general discussion of the following questions . . . (15 min.)

Read a short passage from the scriptures which deals with the theme. Give the students a few moments for personal reflection. (5 min.)

Have the students complete the following statement in their personal journal . . . (10 min.)

Formally dismiss the class. (5 min.)

By breaking your class into time segments, you know exactly what is going to happen and when. This will contribute to your sense of confidence because you know where the class is going. You know how it is to proceed and how it is to end. Also, because you know how much time you have and what you want to do, you are able to be flexible. If something doesn't go the way it was intended to go you can change things around by borrowing from one time segment or extending another. Using time effectively is essential to a well-managed classroom. Plan with an eye on the clock.

Take The Student's Point of View

As you are planning the lesson, keep asking yourself how your students will react. Remember, this lesson was not written with your particular group in mind. Disruptive behavior often occurs when the planned activities are beyond the abilities of the majority of students or, and this is too often the case in religion classrooms, not challenging enough. You need to personalize the lesson — make it fit your group of students. You can do this by keeping the following questions in mind as you prepare your lesson.

- **Is this lesson too sophisticated for my class? Too easy? How can I change it?**
- **What do my students already know about this topic? How can I build on this knowledge? How can I adjust for their lack of knowledge?**
- **Is this suggested activity suited to my students? How do I have to adapt it?**
- **Who in the class will find this an exciting lesson? How can I build on this excitement?**
- **Who in the class will have difficulty with the lesson? How should I adjust for these students?**
- **What questions will this lesson raise for the students? How will I answer them?**
- **How will the students feel about this topic? This lesson? What should I do to deal with their feelings?**

Answering questions like these helps you to put yourself in the mind of the learner. By taking the student's point of view, you are forcing yourself to focus on learning, not on teaching. The answer to the question, "How can the students best learn?" is the answer to the question, "How should I teach?" By answering questions like those above, you are creating a lesson that is geared to *your* students. A lesson that is well matched to the learners is a lesson that will minimize student disruptions. Students will not feel bored or buried. The time and effort you put into planning your lesson from the student's point of view will enhance your effectiveness in creating and maintaining a well-managed classroom.

Know, But Don't Teach, The Theological Background

In your teacher manual, there is usually an introductory section to each lesson that provides you with the theology that informs the lesson plan. You should read this section carefully and if possible discuss it with your DRE and/or other catechists. This theological background is for YOU. By reading this section, you should be able to gain an insight as to why the particular theme of the lesson was selected for the students, and why the written material is not what you are to teach in the lesson. Keep this in mind because there is a tendency at times to want to teach this content to the students. This section is written for the catechist. It's for adults. Its purpose is to inform you. The vocabulary and the concepts are beyond your students.

As you are planning your lesson, don't be asking yourself, "How am I going to insure that they know what I read in the theological introduction?" or "How can I change the lesson so that they will get what I got from the introduction?" These are the wrong questions. You need to know the theology informing the lesson, but you are to teach the lesson designed for the students. The student's lesson will have an outcome that is much different than what you received from reading the theological background. You are an adult, your student is but a child. Lessons are to be geared to the developmental readiness of the learner.

Outline The Lesson

Don't rely on the lesson plan as it is written in the teacher manual. Make the lesson your own. Outline the procedure you are going to use on a 5" x 8" index card. Remember to note the amount of time you are going to devote to each movement. Your outline should not be too elaborate. If it is, it will be more of a hindrance than a help. Keep it brief.

If you have a presentation, this, too, should be outlined. Remember students have short attention spans and are not likely to sit still through a lecture. You need to develop a conversational style in your teaching and the use of an outline can help.

To write your outline read through the material that is suggested in the text, and jot down what you consider to be the main points. A good presentation will try to make no more than 3 or 4 key points. Under each heading put the key thought. The following is an example of an outline for a short presentation on the beatitudes that is to be a part of a fourth grade lesson plan.

Class Presentation

St. Paul wrote letters
- Open Bible Philippians 2:5
    (paraphrase)
"Develop attitudes like Jesus had."

What is an attitude?
    "the way we think, feel, act"

Beatitudes are important
    "guides to the way we should think, feel, act"

(Adapted from Sadlier Fourth Grade Text)

Your presentation can also be written on an index card. Using your index card, rehearse what you are going to say. Keep in mind the amount of time you have to work with. Usually you should take no more than 5 or 10 minutes for a presentation, depending on the age of the students, before you involve them by asking questions, getting feedback or returning to an activity.

Have What You Need

Knowing what supplies you will need is a must particularly on the lower elementary levels. A kingdom can be lost for want of a horse; a well-managed classroom can be lost for want of one extra textbook or a pair of scissors or sharpened pencils or a movie screen. Almost all of today's approved religion textbook series are activity oriented. This means you are going to need supplies. In planning your lesson either formally or informally you should be sure to note what will be required and whether or not you can obtain it. If your lesson is built around Lionni's book *Frederick,* you need to be sure you have a copy in hand. Don't depend on someone bringing it the morning of class. If you're making Ten Commandment posters, make sure you have enough posterboard, glue, magazines and whatever else is called for. If not, you're in for trouble.

The importance of knowing what supplies you'll need is one of the more compelling reasons to start your lesson planning early in the week. You don't want to open you teacher manual on Friday evening at 9:00 to find out that you need a dozen milk cartons and a large piece of felt for tomorrow morning's 8:30 class. Having all of the supplies that are necessary and knowing that they are in working order is essential to creating and maintaining a well-managed classroom. Effective teachers make it a point to do in advance any of the projects that they are going to have the students do. This takes time, but it insures that you know what is involved, what supplies you will need, and where the rough spots are. This also gives you a better indication of the amount of time to allocate for the activity, realizing, of course, that children will work more slowly than an adult. By doing the project in advance, you may realize that you will need some mothers and fathers to be in class to help as aides. Again, have what you need to insure a safe and secure classroom where learning may take place. With good planning you can do it.

Use Your Own Words

Put directions for class activities into your own words. Do not read them to the students from the teacher manual. This will take practice, but it is worth the effort. If you have young children at home, practice on them. If not, get a hold of a niece, nephew or the child next door. A well-managed classroom is dependent on clear and concise instructions. If instructions are not clear, everyone will be mumbling their own to their neighbors. You know you have clear and concise instructions if you can give the directions in your own words. This also indicates to the students that you are in charge. You know what is to be done and how it is to be done. You are not dependent on a book.

List Your Learning Outcomes

This should be one of the first things you do. Before you even begin your outline make a listing of what the students should be able to know, feel or do as a result of participating in this class session. Use your own words. It may be helpful to use the action verbs on pages 52-53 in making your list. Be realistic! Two or three outcomes for any session is the limit. Keep this list in mind as you continue your planning. A good way to write your learning outcomes is to ask yourself, "How should the student answer the parent's question, 'What did you learn in class today?' "

State How You Will Evaluate the Effectiveness of Your Lesson

Planned activities are sometimes successful and at other times they bomb. In planning your lesson state in action verbs those activities of the students that will indicate to you that the class session was successful. Write these indicators of success on the back of the index card with your lesson plan on it. These statements should be directly related to your learning outcomes. If one of your learning outcomes is that the students will compose a personal prayer, an evaluation of the success of the planned lesson is to determine if all of the students will have written a personal prayer. Develop the skill for specifying learning outcomes. With this skill, you will be in a better position for evaluating your effectiveness. You can do it.

Successful teachers are effective teachers. Effective teachers are teachers whose students learn. Evaluation is a systematic process for comparing what you intended to happen with what actually happened in order to improve the lesson in the future. After every class you will make a judgment as to whether or not the class was successful. In a well managed classroom, the teacher knows what to look for because he or she knows what the lesson intended to do. At the end of class turn your lesson plan card over and see if your indicators of success have been met. Always write down how you will evaluate the effectiveness of your lessons. In time you will be not only a proficient evaluator but an effective catechist.

Be A Creative Evaluator

Evaluations don't have to be sophisticated, and they certainly don't have to be written tests or exams. You are a natural evaluator. Use your talent. If your lesson plan is designed to help the students appreciate that the God of our Tradition is a happy God, you could have all of the children at the end of the class or at the end of a series of classes draw a picture of God. Do the majority of pictures indicate that the students view God as happy? If you intend that the students know the Our Father by the 5th week of class, ask the parent(s) to work with the child and send a note indicating that the prayer is known. In preparing your fourth grade class for Reconciliation, your lessons may have stressed that sin is when we turn away from God and do not answer God's call to love others as Jesus loves us. To evaluate this, you might ask the priests who celebrate the sacrament if this was the understanding that was evident in the children. Use your creative abilities.

In Conclusion

A well-planned lesson is essential to a well-managed class-room. Preparing a lesson takes time, not just an hour the night before, much less a few minutes before class is to begin. If you find that this is the case, then you should probably not be a catechist. You don't have the time. Or if you do have the time, you don't have the discipline. But if you've read this far, time and discipline are not your problems. All you need is to follow the suggestions given.

If you view being a catechist as a vocation, teaching will become a part of your life. If you find the subject matter interesting, it is likely that your students will. If you understand why it is necessary to learn the subject matter, it is likely that your students will. If you take a personal interest in preparing your lessons, it is likely that your students too will become personally involved. Preparing a lesson is an act of creation. Be creative!

8
GETTING STARTED

I am falling off a mountain,
I am plummeting through space,
you may see this does not please me
by the frown upon my face.

As the ground keeps getting nearer,
it's a simple task to tell
that I've got a slight dilemma,
that my day's not going well.

My velocity's increasing,
I am dropping like a stone,
I could do with some assistance,
is there someone I can phone?

Though I'm unafraid of falling,
I am prompted to relate
that the landing has me worried,
and I don't have long to wait.

I am running out of options,
there's just one thing left to try —
in the next eleven seconds,
I have go to learn to fly!

Jack Prelutsky
The New Kid on the Block

What Are The Things I Can Do To Get Off To A Good Start?

Good question. You certainly don't want your grand entrance into the classroom to be your first and last step off a mountain. The following suggestions can prevent this. They are suggestions that come from experienced catechists. If used, they can prevent the plummeting feeling that many a catechist has experienced on the first day. There is no need for you to have to declare after entering the classroom, "I've got a slight dilemma, that my day's not going well." There are options.

Have a Seating Arrangement

While not all teachers would agree that a seating arrangement is necessary, it is generally agreed that new teachers are best served by having one. There are a number of reasons for this. A seating arrangement facilitates the learning of the students' names. As was stated earlier, you can't establish an ordered environment if you can't call the students by their names. "Hey, you, don't talk," is not as effective as "Billy, this is a time for quietly working on your poster." A seating arrangement should be written out and kept in a visible spot on your desk or lectern. This will assure you of putting the right name with the right child. It is disconcerting to teacher and student alike when an individual is called by the wrong name. It is also very difficult to learn the right name once you've misnamed a student.

A seating arrangement helps younger students to feel secure and wanted because you've planned for them. It is consoling to have the teacher say, "Oh, Rebecca, I've been waiting for you. Here is your desk." As a catechist, you are with these students for such a short period of time each week that it is imperative that you learn their names as quickly as possible.

In planning your seating arrangement, you might consider alternating boys and girls. You could go down your list alphabetically or randomly select students from your class list. It is helpful to check with your DRE or with catechists from the previous year to find out if there are any students or groups of students who deserve special attention and thus require special seating. There may be students who have hearing difficulties or other types of physical handicaps and need to be near the presentation area. Also, there may be well-known misbehavers. If so, you should see to it that they are seated in places that will facilitate their learning, and in the case of misbehavers that will curb their unacceptable behavior. These students should have seats that are closer to you, the catechist.

In planning your seating arrangement, you may discover that there is a student or students in your class whose presence you think may be problematic. You may know them from the neighborhood, perhaps there is a tension between your families, or you may feel intimidated by the parent or the child. I would suggest that you let your DRE know and that you ask that, if possible, the student(s) be put in another class. You are a catechist, not a professional teacher who has the time and the training to deal with special problems. It is best to take preventative measures before classes ever begin.

Draw your seating arrangement on a large piece of heavy stock paper so that it is durable and you can write in the names in large print. The following illustration shows how you might design your seating plan so that it is easily read from your desk or the lectern in the front of the class.

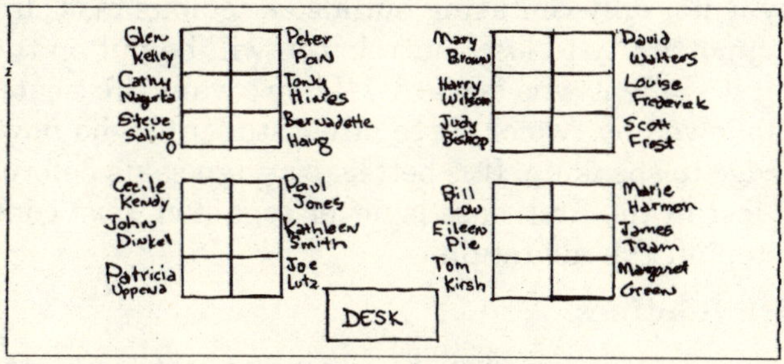

Classroom Seating Chart

Prepare Name Tags

The value of name tags was discussed in an earlier chapter. However, it bears repeating that they are invaluable for catechists. You have a limited amount of time with the students which militates against your learning names quickly, and a well-managed classroom depends on your being able to call each child by name. With the younger student a large piece of cardboard with his or her first name on it and a piece of yarn so that it can be hung around the neck or a creatively designed tag that you can pin on each student as he or she arrives for class works well. For the first meeting you should also have names on the desks so that each student can find his or her desk easily. In larger classes of younger students, it is helpful to have an aide at your first session. After you greet the student at the door and give him or her a name tag, the aide can assist in finding his or her place.

For older students you could have their names on the desks along with a blank name tag and a marker. After you greet them, ask them to find the desk with their name on it and to write their name; they should stay at their desk and talk quietly with their new neighbors until class begins. An aide is also helpful on the upper levels, but not as necessary.

It is important to have every student at his or her assigned desk before class begins; otherwise, you need to take class time to do it. Attempting to assign seats at the start of class on the first day is not only confusing but also a tedious task. It is the perfect opportunity to lose control. You will be put on the spot by the first student who declares, "I don't want this seat." This will be followed by two or three other students who now have the courage to speak up. It is better to assign seats beforehand. Control lost in the first class is never regained. Lost control is a sure step off the mountain.

Establish Routines

It has been emphasized that learning is best facilitated in a well-ordered classroom. To have an ordered classroom you yourself must know the routines that will be followed in your class-room. The following student questions and the suggested answers will help you in establishing your classroom procedures. Read through them and adapt them to your situation.

Student Question: What am I supposed to do when I first enter the classroom?

Suggested Answer: Normally you should greet the students at the door. Welcome them. Have them go to their seats where they are allowed to talk quietly until class begins. Some catechists have activities that the students are to do. These are placed on the students' desks before class or handed to them when they enter. They are then to go to their desks and quietly do the assigned activity. In either case, the students know what's expected of them when they arrive for class. Students should not be allowed to run around, to write on the board, to go in and out of the classroom, or to be loud and rowdy. By not allowing these to happen, you will save yourself the trouble of having to spend the first fifteen minutes of class time re-establishing order in the classroom, a nearly impossible task.

Student Question: How do I address the teacher?

Suggested Answer: It is best to use a title. Let the students know that you are to be called Miss, Mrs., or Mr. Take the time to write your name on the board and to help the students to pronounce it properly. If you have a name that is difficult to pronounce, you might consider shortening it, particularly in the lower elementary grades. But still retain your title. You're asking for trouble if you tell the children to call you by your first name. You want to create a friendly environment conducive to learning in your classroom; this can occur only if you have clearly defined roles. The use of a title helps the students to distinguish roles.

Student Question: What do I do if I want to talk?

Suggested Answer: When you are having a class discussion or presentation the best rule is to tell the students that if they want to talk or to ask a question they are to raise a hand and wait to be called on. When you call on a student, always use his or her name. In small groups, it is best if this same procedure is followed. If a student speaks out without raising a hand, gently remind the student that he or she should raise a hand and that you will call on him or her when it's time. Make sure that you don't call on the same students all the time. Also encourage those students who seldom or never raise their hands to share their comments. You can do this by gently asking those who don't have their hands up if they have anything to say.

Student Question: What do I do if I want to leave the classroom?

Suggested Answer: Because your time with the students is limited, you should let the students know that they should take care of personal needs before coming to class. However, if the need should arise where a student must leave to go to the lavatory, the same procedure as above should be used. The student should raise a hand and ask to be excused. Be sensitive to a student's personal needs, and try to avoid embarrassment. If a student raises his or her hand in the middle of an activity, try to move closer to the student and quietly ask what he or she needs. In this way you save the child from embarrassment and avoid disrupting the whole class. At times, a simple nod from you will suffice. Make sure that the students know where the lavatories are.

As a general rule, only one student at a time should be allowed to go to the lavatory. Beware, once one student leaves for the lavatory, everyone's bladder seems to fill. Unless it is an obvious emergency, if a second student asks to use the lavatory right after the first, he or she can be gently told to wait a few minutes or that class is almost over and he or she can be the first to leave. If you don't control trips to the lavatory, it can become a game. Again, in the first class let the students know that they should take care of their personal needs before coming to class.

Student Question: What am I supposed to do during class activities?

Suggested Answer: Most of the approved catechetical texts today involve the students in a number of activities in the course of a class session. This usually requires a great deal of movement in the classroom. To avoid confusion, you should clearly specify how you are going to hand out supplies for an activity, how the students are to go about grouping themselves for the activity, and how they are to behave in their groupings. These directions are going to vary depending on the activity and the type of classroom in which you are teaching. The important thing is that you know exactly what is to happen and that the students know that they are always to wait for your directions. It is at this point that many catechists lose control. You must know exactly what is to happen and communicate it to the students. Most teacher manuals provide rather specific directions. Read them. Adapt them to your setting. Put them into your own words. Practice giving the directions to others until they are clear.

Student Question: How do I leave the classroom?

> **Suggested Answer:** Leaving the classroom should not be an unplanned activity. Students should not be allowed to take off running at the bell or when the clock indicates that class is over. The students should be told that class is not over until you say it is over. This means that you should be very conscious of ending class on time, but it also means that you, not the bell or the clock, are responsible for dismissing the students. You are there to teach a lesson, and class ends when the lesson is completed. The students should know that they are dismissed when you say they are dismissed.

Your answers to each of these student questions should be incorporated into your class rules. Refer to Chapter Five which deals with class procedures.

What Do I Do On the First Day?

The old saying that first impressions are lasting is nowhere truer than in the classroom. Your first session can make or break the school year. Don't panic; plan. The first session must be a good one. Whatever happens in this session will set the tone for the whole year. The following suggestions will help insure that you and your students start off on the right foot.

Dress Neatly

Clothes don't make the person, but they do influence how the person is perceived. When a student first sees you, he or she will make a judgment based solely on appearances: "Oh, she looks nice." "Hmm, I think I'll like him." "That's a teacher?!" You can't control the student's thoughts, but you can control how you look. Your appearance should indicate that you are neat, well-organized and in control. This doesn't mean you need a new wardrobe, simply that you dress for the occasion. You're not going to a formal party nor to a picnic. A great deal of teaching is modeling. The way you dress models the type of classroom environment you want to create. The type of environment you desire should be neither too formal nor too relaxed. Dress to teach.

Arrive Early

You should arrive early for every class. Stop by the office to let them know that you have arrived and to find out if there is anything you should be aware of for the class that day (announcements, handouts, etc.). Go to your classroom. The following things should be checked:

- Is the room properly arranged for today's class?
- Is the room warm or cool enough?
- Are the supplies ready?
- Are there enough textbooks and supplies?
- Are the lights on?

On the first day, make sure you have all of the name tags. Review the names. If you put names on the desks, make sure that they are on the right desks. You're ready!

Greet the Students

Position yourself by the entrance to your classroom. Greet each student as he or she arrives: "Hello, what is your name?" "Welcome, Billy, I am Mrs. Campbell, and I'll be your teacher this year. Here is your name tag. Find your desk and sit down. You can talk quietly at your desk until I start class. I'm glad you're going to be in my class." You should greet older students in a similar manner. Be sure you are wearing your name tag.

Don't be shy. You will be nervous; there is nothing you can do about that. Act like the type of catechist you want to be: confident. By the fourth or fifth child it will be easy.

Don't leave the doorway to mix with a few students. You need to greet each student individually and to let him or her know that you're glad he or she is in your class. Each student is important to you, and each student must know this from the first moment he or she enters the room. The students must also know that you are the teacher and that you are in charge.

Introduce Yourself

Before you formally begin the lesson, take some time to tell the students who you are. This should be a well rehearsed (not memorized) introduction. Again, you will be nervous but that's okay. Say who you are with enthusiasm, tell what you do during the day, some of your interests and why you are excited about this class. This introduction must model the fact that you are the teacher, you are confident, you know what is going to happen, and you are enthused.

When you are introducing yourself, don't try to be funny or to convince the students that you are their friend. This will only backfire. You want them to know that you are their teacher and that you and they are here to learn. Learning can be fun, but only if the students are in a safe and secure environment. This introduction is your first formal attempt to convey that your classroom is such an environment.

If your class is small enough (no more than 10 or 12 students), you might ask the students to introduce themselves. Be sure to be directive, "Now I would like each of you to introduce yourself to me and to your classmates. We will move around the room. When it is your turn, stand and give your name."

Review Class Procedures

After you've completed the introductions, spend a few minutes explaining class procedures. Stand next to the poster that you made. Read the procedures aloud and make a comment on each. Your explanation should not be long and drawn out. Conclude your explanation by telling the students that if they are unsure about what they should do, they can refer to this poster which will always be on display.

Faithfully Follow You Lesson Plan

Now you are ready to put into effect all the planning that has occurred since you decided to teach this class. Don't panic. Take a deep breath and begin. Be faithful to your outline.

Formally Dismiss the Class

Have a procedure for ending the class. Don't just say that's it. Let the students know that the class period is coming to an end. This is best done by planning five minutes at the end of the period to do the following:

- Summarize what was done in class. (A good way to summarize is to have a short answer to the parent's question, "What did you do in class today?")

- Distribute any handouts you may have and tell the students how they are to be used. Be very specific.

- Thank the students for their participation and tell them you are looking forward to seeing them next week. Give them some idea of what you will be doing in the coming session. Make it sound interesting.

- If books are to be returned before students leave or if furniture is to be put back in place, students should be told the procedure for doing this, and you should be faithful in carrying out the procedure. With younger children, don't just say, "Put your books in the box when you leave," and then go on to another task. You or an aide should make it a point to stand next to the box and thank the students.

- Dismiss in an ordered fashion. With younger children this can be done by rows or groups. Stand by the door as students are leaving. If a student or students want to talk to you, have them wait until the rest of the class has left.

Your class should end as orderly and well-managed as it began. The same dismissal procedure should be used throughout the year. Make it a general rule never to dismiss class early.

In Conclusion

Entering the classroom should never be like falling off a mountain. And it won't be if you prepare. If you take the time beforehand to insure that things are in order, from knowing names to knowing how the class will be dismissed, you will be safe and secure and so will your students. Unlike the fellow in the poem that began this chapter, you won't find yourself in the unenviable position of having to say to yourself, "in the next eleven seconds, I have got to learn to fly!"

9
HANDLING PROBLEMS

Anything you can do to increase communication in your class will reduce your need to impose order by authority, and reduce the student's need to rebel against that authority. The class will become more a place for listening and learning, and less a place for fighting and antagonism.

John O. Stevens
Awareness

What Do I Do If A Student Misbehaves?

This is a common concern of all teachers and the overriding fear of most new ones. It is a concern worth having, but a fear to be overcome. It is a worthwhile concern because behavior affects not only the student who is misbehaving but all students. If one student misbehaves the whole class is affected. It is a fear to be overcome because if you are too concerned with controlling misbehavior you will never get to teaching. Classroom management is not an end in itself, but a means to an end. That end is more effective teaching and learning.

Much of what is considered misbehavior on the student's part, may not be. In fact, what is often viewed by some teachers as student misbehavior is really the teachers' failure to provide a controlled learning environment and a well-planned lesson geared to the student's needs and developmental readiness. This doesn't mean there are no misbehaving students. There are. But the cause of misbehavior shouldn't always be assumed to be the student.

In this chapter you will be provided with five general principles that will help you prevent misbehavior in your classroom. They are principles which will help you create an environment where both listening and learning can take place. After presenting the principles, common "misbehaviors" found in religious education classrooms will be identified and suggestions given for dealing with them.

What Are The Principles?

Expect Respect

As a teacher you can't demand respect. You can earn it in time. But you must first respect yourself. If you don't think yourself worthy of respectful behavior, the students won't. Your task in the classroom is to teach. If you go about your task in a respectful, purposeful and well planned manner, even if you are a beginner, you are doing your job and deserve respect. Convince yourself of this. Expect it.

Use Your Body

When one student begins to act up, it is important to deal with the student promptly but without drawing the class' attention to the misbehaving individual. If you notice that a student is getting restless or is beginning to annoy the person next to him or her, without any fanfare move closer to the student. Closeness is often enough to discourage misbehavior. Your presence or a light touch on the shoulder can do wonders. Eye contact is another way of letting a child know that what he or she is doing is unacceptable. A stern look may be all that is needed. The important thing is to unobtrusively let the student know that you are present and in charge.

Accentuate The Positive

When you are correcting a student don't say "don't"; say "do." "Billy, we are supposed to be reading our book now." "Suzie, when we want to talk in the group we are supposed to raise our hand. Remember?" By using positive statements, you help the child to know what it is he or she should be doing. In this way, you are not focusing on the misbehavior. It is more important that the student knows what to do, rather than what not to do. In the classroom, there are a lot fewer 'dos' to learn than there are 'don'ts.' Think positively, and your students will.

Don't Overreact

Be calm. You are the person in charge. If you lose control, there is little hope for the class. Dealing with misbehavior and mischief is a part of teaching. Learn to keep your voice well modulated when you are correcting the class. Raising your voice or yelling only has the effect of creating more chaos. Remember you are working with youngsters. The saying, "You're acting like a child," has a basis in fact. Children act like children. They act their age. Expect them to. In most instances, children misbehave in the classroom because they are children, not because they are behavior problems.

When a misbehavior occurs, view it as childish behavior and remind the mischief maker of the proper behavior in your classroom. There will be times when patience is tried to the limit, but these should be few and far between. If you find yourself continually at your wits end, perhaps you are not cut out for classroom teaching. Not everyone is. Remember, your special ministry as a classroom catechist is with children. Don't expect them to be anything other than what they are. Exercise your patience. Stay calm.

Keep Things in Perspective

Nothing is as essential to a well-managed classroom as a well-developed sense of perspective. You need to realize that you and your lessons are not the most influential factor in your students' religious formation.

Faith is best developed through sharing and participating in the faith life of the family and the parish community. The classroom is only one small part of the community experience. This doesn't mean the classroom is unimportant, but it's not the end all and be all of religious formation. There are people who will never be able to do well in classroom settings; this does not mean they are incapable of being religious persons. Trust the Spirit. Do everything you can to be the very best classroom catechist you can be. Then sit down in a chair and smile. You might even chuckle.

If you can keep things in perspective, you will be less frustrated in your efforts to become a good catechist. More importantly, you will find yourself being more patient with your students and more understanding of the fact that they are children trying to survive in a classroom, just as you are an adult trying to do the same thing only as a catechist not as a student. It isn't easy. At times, it's even funny. Keep it in perspective.

What Are The Common Problems?

Classrooms have been around for some time, and there are not too many problems that are new. The following are common problems that occur in most parish catechetical programs. The solutions proposed are those that have been used in various parishes and have proven effective. Keep them in mind. Should you encounter any of the problems in your classroom, using these solutions you can act promptly to remedy them. Problems are a part of teaching. View them as a challenge and not as a burden. Again, you are working with youth in a setting that most of them would choose not to be in, if they had a choice.

Walking Into A Noisy Classroom

This the most common problem that parish catechists encounter, and it is one of the easiest to correct. By arriving early and greeting the students at the door when they arrive and having them go to their desks to talk quietly until you start class, you can prevent this problem. This is an arrival procedure you should initiate on the very first day of class. If you have a particularly active group, you might have some type of paper and pencil activity or a reading assignment on the desk for the students to complete before class begins.

A Student Continually Coming Late To Class

In the lower grades this is usually not the fault of the child but of the parent. A phone call to the parent by you or the DRE is usually enough to resolve the problem. Let the parent know that by arriving late the child is missing out on a key part of the lesson and disturbing the rest of the class. Stress that because there is so little time for class it is important that each child be on time. If the problem persists, let the DRE know. Perhaps, he or she can arrange some type of plan with the parent whereby the child can arrive on time.

Forgetting Textbooks Or Homework

Forgetting a textbook is a normal problem when you allow textbooks to go home. To solve the problem you could keep the textbooks in the classroom and not allow them to be taken home. This is a drastic move because there is a value in providing the parent with an opportunity to look at the child's text. The other option is to have extra textbooks in the classroom.

Homework is always going to be a problem in a program that meets only once a week and that has no external incentives like grades for passing or failing the course. If you are going to have homework, it is probably best to assign it occasionally. If your class is small enough, call the students the day before to remind them that there is class the next day and they shouldn't forget their homework. It is a good policy never to plan your lesson around students' homework. If the homework isn't done, your lesson is in jeopardy.

A Bad Attitude

Every once in awhile you will get a student in your class who does not want to be there. There may be many reasons for this attitude. As soon as you notice a student like this, you should talk to him or her after class. If things improve, fine. If not, talk to your DRE. You are not a professional teacher, and even if you were you do not have enough time in a parish program to deal with a student's personal problems. The DRE should provide some other option for the student. Problem students should not be your problem. You have enough to do in becoming a proficient catechist with the normal classroom concerns.

This solution doesn't mean you're not interested in the student's well-being. It simply means you're not the person to deal with his or her problem. Your responsibility as a classroom catechist is to the group. You must maintain a learning environment that allows each individual to learn in a group setting. If you have a student who is preventing this by his or her attitude, he or she must be removed for the good of the other individuals.

Doing Work Poorly

Because most catechetical programs do not assign students to classes on the basis of learning abilities, you normally have students in your classroom with a wide range of skills. This is problematic. You are responsible for choosing activities that will appeal to all of the individuals in your class. If the range of abilities is too diverse this becomes an impossibility. What one student finds challenging, another may find tedious and vice versa. When this occurs, your classroom is a perfect environment for disciplinary problems.

If you find that your classroom is such an environment, it would be good to employ the services of a catechist-aide or aides. The aides can assume responsibility for assisting those students who are having difficulty completing a project or activity or who have completed the work and are looking for something to do. The use of aides on the elementary level is highly recommended.

The objection that comes most often from catechists concerning the use of aides is, "I wouldn't feel comfortable having someone else in the room." You may feel the same way. No one can take away the fear, but knowing that in those classrooms where there are aides the disciplinary problems are drastically reduced should give you pause for reflection. You are teaching so that students may learn. Aides are extremely valuable in the teaching/learning process. They allow for more individual attention in the classroom setting. Don't rule them out. Your students may need them.

Lack Of Class Participation

This is the disciplinary problem ignored by most teachers. Most of a teacher's disciplinary attention goes to those students who are acting up not to those who aren't acting. The student who never becomes involved is easy to ignore because he or she isn't disrupting the whole class. However, failure to participate is a disciplinary problem. If you notice that you have a student who is withdrawn, gently encourage him or her to become involved. "Johnny, would you help put out the supplies with Mark." "Sylvia, you have a nice picture here; would you hold it up for the class?" Don't put the child on the spot, but do provide opportunities for involvement. This can be done by directing a question to the student. You might even say something to the child before or after class encouraging him or her to become involved. Let the child know that you are confident that he or she has something of value to share with the class. If the problem persists you should mention it to your DRE. A call to a parent might be in order.

There are times, especially with seventh and eighth grade students, when you will feel like the whole class is in a state of non-participation. They are. It is part of being a seventh or eighth grader. In classrooms, seventh and eighth graders seem to be either chaotic or catatonic. Don't view it as a character disorder. It's just their age. It is an age that demands that you use all of your creative skills as a teacher, but doesn't offer any rousing response for your efforts. They are learning. You can't force participation. You need to bring your own enthusiasm and in time participation will come. To work with this age you need to be comfortable with yourself.

Not Enough Class Time

If this is the case, you are the problem. You are not working to the clock when you plan your lessons. Or if you are working to the clock, you have an unrealistic perception of the amount of time classroom activities take. The best solution to this problem is to plan your lessons with a person who has a better sense of the time involved in classroom activities. Don't get discouraged. Working to the clock is a skill. It may take time, but you can develop it.

The Students Won't Listen

If you have an exceptionally unruly grouping, there is not much you can do. The task for the year will be to make the best of a bad situation. It will be a tough year. By year's end you will be an exhausted but much wiser classroom teacher. However, when students won't listen it usually isn't the fault of the students, but a failure on the part of the teacher. The teacher has failed to establish his or her authority. There is a problem when this happens early in the year. Sad to say, there is very little that can be done to regain the lost control.

If this is your situation and the class is totally out of hand, it may be best if you let someone else teach the class. This doesn't mean you're not a teacher, but it does indicate that you are going to have to work on your classroom management skills. It would be good if you could spend some time as an aide to a skilled classroom manager. Believe it or not you will be better the next time you teach. Don't look on your stepping down as a failure but as a learning experience. Think of the little girl who has learned, she replied, "Oh, by getting up every time I fell down."

These are the problems that occur most frequently in parish religious education programs. You can't prevent all of them, but you can know what to do when they occur.

In Conclusion

Students are not perfect, just as catechists are not perfect. Problems are a part of teaching. Don't get discouraged by them. They are challenges. Challenges are opportunities for growth. Take them on. You'll be a better catechist. But keep in mind that the problems you are to deal with are the problems of the classroom and not the problems of the home. If there are problems outside the classroom that are affecting the behavior of a student in your classroom, let the DRE know. He or she will handle it from there. Your task is to create a classroom environment in which both teaching and learning can prosper.

10
PULLING IT ALL TOGETHER

Apollinaire said, "Come to the edge."

"We might fall."

"Come to the edge."

"It's too high."

COME TO THE EDGE

> *And they come.*
> *And you push them.*
> *And they fly.*

Maria Harris
Portrait of Youth Ministry

How Can I Keep It Going?

Throughout this book we've talked about the importance of developing successful classroom management skills. You've been given many strategies for bettering yourself as a classroom catechist. As you've been able to tell, much of what it takes to be successful depends upon how positively you think about yourself. In almost every chapter, you've seen how a positive approach can help improve. If you're going to be effective in the classroom, if your students are going to learn, if you're going to be faithful to your catechetical task of "echoing" the word of God in a way that will help your students' faith become living, conscious and active, you've got to believe you can do it. You've been given a push, and you can fly!

Effective classroom management is the result of a well-planned interaction between the teacher, the learner, the learning environment, and the subject matter. If these four elements are working together, the result is a classroom in which the teacher teaches and the learner learns. If you continue to apply the principles and suggestions provided in this book, you will continue to be a successful classroom manager and an effective catechist. The following is a brief summary of what has been written. Throughout the year refer to it as a checklist. It will recall to mind those things that you should be doing in your classroom to remain a successful classroom manager.

The summary is divided into four sections: Teacher, Student, Classroom and Subject Matter.

The Teacher

Think positively. You've prepared in many ways for teaching; now you are ready. Your chances of success are excellent. Have a positive self-image. Dress and act like the effective catechist that you are.

Plan ahead. Use both formal and informal planning. Planning takes time, but it's time well spent. Plan well and there will be little opportunity for class disruption.

Visualize. Picture yourself in the classroom. Rehearse each class session in your mind. Imagine the rough spots and iron them out. Don't enter the classroom "cold." Think it through.

Focus on learning, not teaching. Concern yourself with learning outcomes. What are the students to know, to feel or to do? It will then be easier to answer the question, "How should I teach?"

Be enthusiastic. Let the students know that you are interested in what you teach and that you enjoy teaching. Enthusiasm is catching.

Learn to laugh. If you can't laugh at yourself and the situations you will find yourself in as a classroom catechist, you shouldn't teach. Teaching is serious business. Learning is fun. Humor ties the two together. A healthy sense of humor puts things into perspective.

The Student

Respect the student. Each student is a unique person. Learn names. Be aware of personal strengths and weaknesses and give attention to learning styles. Let the student know that he or she is special, and special behavior will follow.

Focus on the whole person. Your students are thinking, feeling, acting individuals. Develop each dimension of their personalities. Use a balanced approach in planning and teaching your lessons.

Keep expectations high. Students will live up to your expectations if the expectations are reasonable and if you encourage and trust them to do so. Speak in an affirming and challenging manner.

State your expectations. Students will feel more secure and ready to learn if they know what is expected of them. Outline your lessons and tell the students where you are going. Specify classroom procedures and post them. When you correct a student state the proper behavior expected.

Be honest. Encourage students to ask their religious questions and the questions about religion. Be clear and straight forward in your response. If you can't answer or don't have an answer, say so. Assist the students in finding their own answers.

Observe confidentiality. What happens in the classroom should ordinarily stay there. Students will feel more secure and freer to speak and to question if they know that what they say will not be repeated or used against them.

The Classroom

Develop a feel for the room. Your classroom is where you'll perform your ministry as catechist. Visit it early. Plan ways to adapt it to your needs and to your teaching style. Be aware of its strengths and weaknesses both physically and emotionally.

Make it functional. Your classroom is to be designed to make your lesson plans work. It should assist the students in learning and you in teaching. Read your teacher manual in order to know what special areas will be needed during the lessons. Then plan your room so that learning can take place. Make the room your own. Design your own floor plan.

Make the room a teaching tool. You have the students for a short time during the year. This time must be used productively. Creative use of bulletin boards, chalkboards and posters can serve as visual cues, reminders, and lesson reviews. The proper arrangement of desks and tables can create an environment that teaches as it invites students to learn.

Make the classroom visually appealing. Don't overdecorate. Do let the students know that you prepared for them. Have bulletin boards, desks, Bible stands, etc. neat and attractive. Your classroom should be a comfortable place for teaching and learning.

Have a place for everything and everything in its place. An orderly classroom gives students the feeling that someone is in control and that learning can take place. Also if everything is in place, time won't be wasted looking for things and there will be less chance of students misbehaving.

The Subject Matter

Set aside time for lesson planning. No one can be a successful teacher if he or she does not plan for class. Set up a schedule so that you have time to both informally and formally plan your lessons. Use the teacher manual and be aware of its catechetical process. Don't fall into the trap of leaving your lesson planning to the night before.

Take the student's point of view: Remember you are teaching for learning. Each student and each class is unique. Your lesson plans, while designed for students at the same age level as yours, have to be adapted to the students in your class.

Outline the lesson. A good way to become comfortable with a lesson is to outline it. In this way, the lesson will become a part of you. In planning your lesson remember to work to the clock. This is a key to successful classroom management. You don't want your lessons to be too long nor too short.

Have what you need. Plan ahead. Have everything you need before you enter the classroom. Don't be rushing around at the last minute looking for supplies. Teaching is a planned activity.

List your learning outcomes. The purpose of teaching is change, change for the better. This change may take place on the cognitive, affective or behavioral level. In order to clarify what you want to happen in your classroom, write out your learning outcomes using action verbs to indicate the desired changes.

Evaluate. Since your purpose is to teach so that students may learn, it is important to find out if any learning took place. Using your listing of learning outcomes, indicate what behaviors of the students will let you know that your lesson was effective, that the students learned. The only way you can improve as a catechist is to know whether or not you were effective.

In Conclusion

To be a successful manager you must believe that you can be one. You must act like one. You must have trust in your own abilities. Our goal in this book is to give you three things. We want you to realize that you can become a successful catechist and an effective classroom manager if you work at it. Secondly, we want to motivate you to put forth the effort that is needed to become both. Lastly, we want to provide you with some practical guides that will help you in your efforts to be a successful catechist and an effective classroom manager. We've come to the end; it's up to you now.

Come to the edge.
    You won't fall.

Come to the edge.
    It's not too high.

Come to the edge.
    Don't be afraid.

COME TO THE EDGE!

    YOU CAN FLY!

ACKNOWLEDGMENTS

QUOTATIONS

Frederick by Leo Lionni (New York: Pantheon, 1967)

Alice in Wonderland by Lewis Carroll (New York: New American Library, 1960) p. 62.

Attributed to no source. Cited in *100 Ways to Enhance Self-Concept in the Classroom* by Jack Canfield and Harold C. Wells (New Jersey: Prentice-Hall, 1976) p. 182.

The Complete Works of Ralph Waldo Emerson. Cited in *100 Ways to Enhance Self-Concept in the Classroom* by Jack Canfield and Harold C. Wells (New Jersey: Prentice-Hall, 1976) p. 38.

Pygmalion by George Bernard Shaw. Cited in *100 Ways to Enhance Self-Concept in the Classroom* by Jack Canfield and Harold C. Wells (New Jersey: Prentice-Hall, 1976) p. 100.

The Art of Teaching by Gilbert Highet (New York: Vintage Books, 1950) p. 25.

Discourses by Epictitus. Cited in *100 Ways to Enhance Self-Concept in the Classroom* by Jack Canfield and Harold C. Wells (New Jersey: Prentice-Hall, 1976) p. 173.

the little red school book by Soren Hansen and Jesper Jensen (New York: Pocket Books, 1973) pp.26-27.

The New Kid on the Block by Jack Prelutsky (New York: Greenwillow Books, 1984) p. 149.

Awareness by John O. Stevens. Cited in *100 Ways to Enhance Self-Concept in the Classroom* by Jack Canfield and Harold C. Wells (New Jersey: Prentice-Hall, 1976) p. 145.

Portrait of Youth Ministry by Maria Harris. Cited in *DRE: Issues and Concerns for the 80s* edited by Thomas P. Walters (Washington, DC: National Conference of Diocesan Directors of Religious Education, 1983) p. 31.